Byte Rich:
The Bitcoin Odyssey

By: Jeff Alan

Summary:

"Byte Rich: The Bitcoin Odyssey" is a coming-of-age story set against the backdrop of the early days of Bitcoin.

Alex, a high school student with a passion for technology, discovers Bitcoin and is quickly drawn into its revolutionary potential.

As Alex delves deeper into the world of cryptocurrency, he encounters challenges and opportunities that shape his journey from a novice enthusiast to a mature entrepreneur.

Alongside his friends Sarah and Liam, Alex navigates the complex landscape of digital currency, learning about technology, finance, and the value of perseverance and ethical decision-making.

Detailed Chapter Breakdown and Storyline:

1. **Genesis Block**: Alex's introduction to Bitcoin is depicted through his stumbling upon a forum discussing Satoshi Nakamoto's whitepaper. He's captivated by the idea of a decentralized currency and begins to research how he could be a part of this new world.

2. **Into the Blockchain**: Alex successfully mines his first Bitcoin on a rudimentary PC setup. This chapter serves as an educational introduction to Bitcoin mining, explaining the basics in a way accessible to young adults.

3. **Blockchain Horizons**: Alex's success catches the attention of his schoolmates. Sarah, intrigued by the economic implications, and Liam, fascinated by the technological aspect, join Alex. This chapter shows the formation of their team and the start of their venture.

4.   **Pooling Resources**: Facing competition from larger miners, the group decides to join a mining pool. This chapter explains how mining pools work and the significance of collaboration in the Bitcoin community.

5.   **Blockchain Pioneers**: At a blockchain conference, the team meets pioneers in the field. They attend workshops and panels, which serve as a medium to introduce readers to broader applications of blockchain technology beyond cryptocurrencies.

6.   **Byte Rich, Byte Wise**: A spike in Bitcoin's value brings unexpected wealth, but also new challenges. The trio must navigate the responsibilities that come with their newfound wealth, exploring themes of financial wisdom, ethics, and the social impact of wealth.

7.   **Scaling New Heights**: As they expand their operation, the group confronts technical challenges and regulatory hurdles, mirroring the real-world evolution of cryptocurrency businesses. This chapter introduces entrepreneurship skills, business planning, and the importance of adapting to a changing environment.

8.   **The Fork in the Road**: A contentious update in the Bitcoin network causes division within the community. The chapter uses this

event to discuss the concept of hard forks, governance in decentralized systems, and the resilience of open-source communities.

9. **Rigging the Game**: The trio upgrades their equipment, assembling their first mining rig from scratch. Detailed descriptions of the hardware and the process provide a deeper understanding of the technology behind Bitcoin mining.

10. **The Value of a Byte**: The characters experience the highs and lows of Bitcoin's value. Discussions among them introduce economic concepts such as market volatility, supply and demand, and the impact of external events on cryptocurrency.

11. **Hack Attack**: A hacking incident at a major Bitcoin exchange introduces the theme of cybersecurity. Alex and his team learn about the importance of secure digital practices, both personally and in the wider Bitcoin network.

12. **Full Circle**: The story culminates with Alex looking back on his journey. The final chapter reflects on the growth of both the characters and the Bitcoin ecosystem, leaving readers with a sense of optimism about the future of cryptocurrencies.

Character Development:

- **Alex**: His journey is one of personal growth, from a curious teenager to a knowledgeable, responsible entrepreneur. His character embodies innovation, adaptability, and ethical decision-making.

- **Sarah**: Brings a critical and analytical perspective, often sparking discussions about the economic and social implications of cryptocurrencies.

- **Liam**: Represents the tech-enthusiast, delving into the technical aspects of Bitcoin and often explaining complex concepts in layman's terms.

Educational Elements:

- Dialogues and narrative that naturally incorporate educational content about Bitcoin and blockchain.

- Subplots involving real-world events and developments in the cryptocurrency space to provide context and authenticity.

- Inclusion of resources and references for readers interested in exploring the topics further.

"Byte Rich: The Bitcoin Odyssey" aims to be a compelling mix of storytelling and education, providing an insightful and engaging exploration of the world of Bitcoin, tailored for young adults.

Chapter 1: Genesis Block

Setting:

- The story begins in a small suburban town, focusing on a typical high school setting.

- The time period is set during the early years of Bitcoin, capturing the essence of a budding digital revolution.

Characters:

- **Alex**: A 16-year-old high school student with a knack for computers and a curious mind. Portrayed as a bit of an outsider, but well-liked by those who know him.

- **Alex's Family**: Supportive but not particularly tech-savvy, providing a contrast to Alex's technological inclination.

- **School Environment**: A backdrop of teachers and students, some of whom will play a larger role in later chapters.

Plot Points:

1. **Discovery of Bitcoin**:

   - Alex stumbles upon an online forum discussing Bitcoin and Satoshi Nakamoto's whitepaper. His curiosity is piqued by the concept of a decentralized digital currency.

2. **Research and Understanding**:

   - Alex spends nights researching Bitcoin, grappling with concepts like blockchain, cryptography, and the philosophy behind decentralization.

   - Incorporate dialogues with friends and family, showcasing his excitement and their skepticism or lack of understanding.

3. **First Steps in Mining**:

   - With resources gathered from online communities and forums, Alex decides to try mining Bitcoin using his old computer.

   - Detailed descriptions of his trial-and-error process, setting up the mining software, and the excitement of participating in the Bitcoin network.

4.   **Encountering Challenges**:

- Alex faces technical challenges, from hardware limitations to software issues.

- He also experiences his first taste of the volatile online community surrounding Bitcoin, learning to navigate differing opinions and information.

5.   **First Success**:

- The climax of the chapter is Alex successfully mining his first fraction of a Bitcoin.

- This moment is a mix of triumph and revelation, as he realizes the potential of what he's engaged in.

6.   **Reflection and Projection**:

- The chapter closes with Alex reflecting on his journey so far and dreaming about the possibilities that Bitcoin could bring.

- A foreshadowing of his ambitions and the challenges he will face.

Chapter 1: Genesis Block

This chapter will set the tone for the rest of the novel, combining storytelling with educational elements about Bitcoin. It's important to maintain a balance between developing the narrative and characters, and providing informative content about the cryptocurrency world. The goal is to leave readers both entertained and informed, eager to follow Alex on his journey in subsequent chapters.

Setting: A crisp autumn evening in a quiet suburban town. The streets are lined with modest homes, and the distant sound of a high school football game echoes faintly.

Characters:

Alex: A 16-year-old with a curious gaze and a penchant for tinkering with electronics.

His room is cluttered with computer parts and tech magazines.

Alex's Family: His mother, a school teacher, and his father, a local mechanic, offer a grounded contrast to Alex's tech-oriented world.

School Friends: Brief mentions of school friends, setting the stage for their later involvement.

Narrative:

Alex sat hunched over his old desktop, the glow of the screen casting long shadows across his room. The hum of the aging processor mixed with the occasional cheer from the distant football game, creating a soundtrack to his intense focus. He had stumbled upon something utterly fascinating, something that echoed the beats of a digital revolution — Bitcoin.

It was a forum post that caught his attention first. "The Future of Money," it read. The words of Satoshi Nakamoto, a name shrouded in mystery, spoke of a decentralized currency, a blockchain. Alex's mind raced with questions. How could a currency exist purely in the digital realm? What was this blockchain?

Night after night, Alex dove into the depths of the internet, piecing together information from forums, articles, and the original Bitcoin whitepaper. He encountered words and concepts that were alien yet intriguing: decentralization, cryptography, digital ledgers.

"Are you coming to dinner, Alex?" his mother's voice cut through his concentration.

"Just a minute," Alex replied, barely glancing away from the screen. His mind was elsewhere, dancing through lines of code and the potential of digital currency.

He learned about Bitcoin mining, a process of validating transactions and creating new Bitcoins. It was a race, a competition, a digital gold rush, and Alex wanted in. With his modest savings, he couldn't afford the latest hardware, but that wouldn't stop him. He would start with what he had — his old desktop.

The first attempt was clumsy. The computer whirred and struggled as Alex navigated through the setup of mining software. Error messages were frequent visitors on his screen. Yet, with each setback, his resolve only strengthened. He was not just a high school student anymore; he was a miner, a pioneer in a new digital frontier.

Days turned into weeks. Alex's initial excitement was met with the reality of his endeavor. Mining was not just a matter of setting up software; it was a battle against odds, against more powerful machines, against a network growing more competitive by the day.

But then, it happened. A fraction of a Bitcoin, minuscule yet monumental, appeared in Alex's digital wallet. The thrill was indescribable — he had mined his first Bitcoin. It was a triumph not of financial gain but of persistence and learning.

As he lay in bed that night, the events of the past few weeks replayed in his mind. He thought about the potential of Bitcoin, not just as a digital currency but as a movement, a challenge to the traditional notions of money and transactions. He imagined the possibilities, not just for himself but for the world.

Little did he know, this was just the beginning. The journey ahead would take him from these quiet nights in his room to places and challenges he couldn't yet fathom. But for now, he slept, a smile faintly playing on his lips, dreaming of a world changed by lines of code and an idea named Bitcoin.

The next morning, Alex's eyes opened to the early rays of sunlight filtering through his blinds. His first thoughts were of the tiny fraction of Bitcoin now sitting in his digital wallet. It was a small victory in the grand scheme, but it felt like a giant leap to him.

At breakfast, Alex couldn't contain his excitement. "I mined Bitcoin!" he exclaimed, his words rushing out in a torrent.

His parents exchanged puzzled looks. "Bit-what?" his father asked, eyebrows furrowed, as he passed the milk.

"It's digital money, Dad. Like, the money of the future!" Alex replied, his spoon forgotten in his cereal bowl.

His mother smiled, her expression a mix of affection and confusion. "That sounds... interesting, dear. Is it safe?"

Alex launched into an explanation, trying to condense nights' worth of research into a few sentences. He talked about blockchain, the security of transactions, and the potential of decentralized currency.

His words were met with nods, but he could tell they didn't fully grasp the concept. It didn't matter, though. He was used to being the tech expert in the family.

School that day was a blur. Alex's mind was on Bitcoin, on the possibilities that lay ahead. During lunch, he shared his success with a couple of friends, but the conversation didn't go as he had hoped.

"Sounds like a scam," one friend commented, shrugging.

"Isn't that for buying illegal stuff on the internet?" another asked, raising an eyebrow.

Frustrated, Alex realized that Bitcoin was still a fringe concept, misunderstood and shrouded in skepticism. He needed to learn more, to be able to explain it better, to show them the potential he saw.

The following weeks were a deep dive into the world of cryptocurrency. Alex joined online communities, participated in forums, and consumed every piece of information he could find. He tweaked his mining setup, optimizing it within the limits of his resources.

But as Alex delved deeper, he also encountered the complexities and controversies surrounding Bitcoin. He read heated debates over its scalability, the environmental impact of mining, and regulatory challenges. He learned about other cryptocurrencies, each with its unique features and communities.

One evening, as he sat at his desk, the reality of what he was embarking on began to dawn on him. Bitcoin was not just a technological marvel; it was a socio-economic experiment, a challenge to the established financial system.

His first successful mining attempt was no longer just a personal achievement; it was a gateway into a world that was complex, fascinating, and constantly evolving.

Alex realized that his journey with Bitcoin was going to be about more than just mining or making money. It was about being part of something revolutionary, something that could change how the world viewed currency and transactions.

He is not just a teenager with a computer anymore. He is a young explorer at the forefront of a digital frontier, ready to face the challenges and opportunities that lay ahead in the uncharted territory of Bitcoin.

The weeks turned into months, and Alex's bedroom transformed into a makeshift command center for his Bitcoin mining operations. The whir of cooling fans became a constant backdrop to his life, a mechanical symphony that played to the rhythm of his growing fascination with cryptocurrency.

One evening, as winter whispered its arrival outside, Alex sat hunched over his keyboard, his face illuminated by the soft glow of dual monitors. He had just joined a heated discussion on an online forum about the future of Bitcoin. The debate was intense, with opinions ranging from wildly optimistic to doom-laden. Alex, with his modest mining setup and earnest enthusiasm, felt like a minnow swimming amongst sharks.

But it was in this ocean of ideas and arguments that Alex began to find his voice. He chimed in, initially with tentative replies that grew in confidence as he marshaled his thoughts and knowledge.

Alex spoke of Bitcoin's potential to democratize financial systems, to provide a haven from unstable national currencies, and to offer a new level of privacy in transactions.

His comments caught the attention of other forum members, some of whom were veterans in the space. One user, going by the handle "CryptoSage," reached out to Alex with a direct message. "You've got a sharp mind, kid. Ever thought about expanding your mining operation?"

CryptoSage introduced Alex to the concept of mining pools, collaborative groups of miners who combined their computational power to compete more effectively in the Bitcoin network. This was a game-changer for Alex. He had reached the limits of what he could achieve with his lone setup; joining a pool could catapult his mining endeavors to new heights.

The next few days were a blur of activity. Alex researched various mining pools, weighing their payout structures, fees, and reputations. He settled on one that seemed a good fit and reconfigured his mining software to join the pool. The shift was dramatic. Where once he had been mining fractions of Bitcoin sporadically, he was now earning more consistently, albeit smaller, shares of the rewards.

This success, however, brought new challenges. His parents began to question the rising electricity bills and the constant hum of the mining rigs that had taken over his room. Alex found himself explaining not just the costs, but the potential long-term benefits of his endeavor.

He talked about the rise in Bitcoin's value and how this could be an investment in his future. His parents, though skeptical, agreed to let him continue, provided he kept up with his schoolwork.

Alex reflects on his journey so far. He had started as a curious teenager dabbling in a new technology, and now he was an active participant in a global financial revolution. The road ahead was uncertain and fraught with technical and ethical dilemmas, but Alex was ready. He had a vision of what Bitcoin could become and a determination to play his part in its evolution.

Alex looking out his bedroom window at the starlit sky, pondering the vastness of the digital universe he had stepped into. He realized that Bitcoin was more than a digital currency; it was a symbol of innovation, a challenge to the status quo, and a testament to the power of human ingenuity.

The snow had begun to fall softly outside, blanketing the neighborhood in a serene white. Inside, however, Alex's room was ablaze with the feverish glow of computer screens, the air tinged with the heat of processors working overtime.

The hum of the fans was a constant reminder of the relentless pursuit of Bitcoin mining.

Alex, now more confident in his role as a miner, started to branch out into other areas of the Bitcoin ecosystem. He began attending local meetups, a gathering of like-minded individuals passionate about cryptocurrency.

It was at one of these meetings that Alex met Maya, a computer science student from a nearby university. Maya's understanding of the technical aspects of blockchain technology was profound, and she introduced Alex to concepts beyond the basics of mining.

Their conversations often spilled over into discussions about the broader implications of Bitcoin. Maya challenged Alex to think about the ethical considerations of cryptocurrency — its potential for both positive change and misuse. These discussions opened a new world for Alex, one where technology intersected with philosophy, economics, and social justice.

Back at home, Alex's parents became increasingly concerned about his obsession with Bitcoin. They worried not only about the tangible costs, like the electricity bill, but also about how this new venture was consuming his life. Alex reassured them that he was managing his school responsibilities, but a growing part of him knew that Bitcoin had become more than just a hobby.

As winter turned to spring, Alex's mining pool began to see diminishing returns. The increasing difficulty of mining and the influx of more powerful, specialized hardware meant that his modest setup was no longer competitive. Faced with this new reality, Alex had to make a decision: either scale up his operation, investing more money and resources, or pivot to another aspect of the cryptocurrency world.

After much thought, Alex decided to transition from mining. He sold his mining rigs to a fellow enthusiast and started exploring other avenues within the Bitcoin space. His interest was piqued by the concept of Bitcoin trading and market analysis.

Alex set up a small trading account, starting with some of the Bitcoin he had mined. He spent hours studying market trends, learning about technical and fundamental analysis, and understanding the impact of global economic news on cryptocurrency markets.

Alex, no longer the wide-eyed teenager who marveled at mining his first Bitcoin. He had matured into a young adult with a nuanced understanding of the cryptocurrency landscape.

His journey had taken him from a lone miner in his bedroom to a participant in a global economic movement. He had learned about the potential and pitfalls of Bitcoin, about the balance of risk and reward, and about the responsibility that came with being part of something as transformative as Bitcoin.

Alex sits at his desk, his eyes reflecting the ever-fluctuating numbers on the trading screen. He is excited, apprehensive, and curious about what the future holds — not just for himself, but for the world of Bitcoin and beyond. The last line of the chapter reads, "In the world of Bitcoin, every end is just a new beginning."

One brisk spring morning, Alex sat at the kitchen table, his laptop open to a trading platform, graphs and numbers flashing across the screen. His father, sipping his coffee, peered over his shoulder.

"What's all this, Alex? Stock market stuff?" his father asked, trying to make sense of the charts.

Alex chuckled, "Sort of, Dad. It's Bitcoin trading. Remember, the digital currency I told you about?"

His father frowned slightly, "Ah, yes, the Bitcoin thing. But trading? Sounds risky."

Alex nodded, understanding his father's concern. "It is, to an extent. But I've learned a lot. It's not just guesswork; there's strategy involved."

His mother, placing a plate of scrambled eggs on the table, joined in, "Just be careful, honey. We don't want you getting in over your head."

Alex reassured them, "I will, Mom. I'm starting small, and I've set strict limits for myself."

The dialogue was interrupted by the chime of a new message on Alex's laptop. It was from Maya, who had become not just a mentor but a close friend.

"Hey Alex, there's a Bitcoin meetup this weekend. Big discussion on the future of blockchain. You in?" the message read.
Alex's fingers flew over the keyboard, "Definitely! Wouldn't miss it."

Maya's reply came quickly, "Great! There's also someone I want you to meet. He's working on a blockchain project for social good. Think you'll be interested."

The prospect of meeting like-minded individuals excited Alex. He had come to realize that the world of Bitcoin was as much about community and shared ideas as it was about technology and finance.

That weekend, at the meetup, Alex and Maya engaged in a lively discussion with a small group of enthusiasts. The air was charged with ideas and debates.

One of the attendees, an older gentleman with a keen eye, turned to Alex, "You're quite young to be so deep in the Bitcoin world. What's your take on the ethical implications of this all?"

Alex pondered for a moment before replying, "I believe Bitcoin has the power to do good. It's a tool, and like any tool, its impact depends on how we use it. The decentralization, the transparency it offers, can be harnessed for social benefit."

Maya chimed in, "He's right. It's not just about making money. We're at the cusp of a financial revolution, and we have the responsibility to steer it in the right direction."

The dialogue around the table grew more animated as ideas were exchanged. Alex felt a sense of belonging, of being part of something important.

As the chapter draws to a close, Alex reflects on his journey so far. The conversations at the meetup had opened his eyes to the broader implications of Bitcoin. He realized that his journey was not just about personal gain but also about understanding the impact of this technology on society.

Alex in a contemplative mood, the moonlight streaming through his window. "Bitcoin is more than a currency; it's a new way of thinking about money and society," he mused. With this thought, he closed his laptop, eager for the challenges and opportunities that awaited him in the ever-evolving world of Bitcoin.

The next day at school, Alex found himself in a conversation with his friend Liam, who had heard about Alex's foray into Bitcoin.
Liam approached Alex by his locker. "Hey, I heard you're into Bitcoin now. That's like, virtual money, right?" he asked, his curiosity piqued.

Alex smiled, eager to share his passion. "Yeah, it's digital currency. It's kind of like the money of the internet. I've been mining and recently started trading it too."

Liam's eyes widened. "Sounds cool, but also kind of complicated. How does it even work?"

Alex launched into an explanation, simplifying the technicalities. "So, Bitcoin runs on this thing called blockchain. It's a ledger, but not like any ledger you've seen before. It's distributed across thousands of computers, so it's really secure and transparent."

"Huh, that actually sounds pretty groundbreaking," Liam admitted, intrigued. "But is it safe? I mean, it's not like regular money."

"That's the thing," Alex replied, leaning against his locker, "It's different from traditional money, but that's what makes it interesting. It's decentralized, no banks or governments control it, and transactions are anonymous."

Liam nodded thoughtfully. "Anonymous transactions? Sounds like it could be used for the wrong reasons too."

Alex nodded. "True, it's not perfect. But it's not the currency that's good or bad; it's about how people use it. And the potential for good is enormous."

Their conversation was cut short by the bell, signaling the end of the school day. As they parted ways, Liam called out, "Let's talk more about this, yeah? I want to understand it better."

Walking home, Alex's mind buzzed with ideas. His conversation with Liam made him realize how much he enjoyed explaining Bitcoin to others. It wasn't just about the technology or the trading; it was about sharing knowledge and perspectives.

That evening, Alex received a message from Maya. "Hey, there's a blockchain startup looking for young, tech-savvy individuals. Thought you might be interested."

Alex's heart skipped a beat. This was an opportunity to get even more involved in the world of cryptocurrency. "Definitely interested! Thanks for thinking of me, Maya," he quickly replied.

Alex sits at his desk, reflecting on his journey. He had started as a curious teenager exploring Bitcoin, and now he was on the brink of diving into something even bigger. He realized that his adventure was just beginning, and there was so much more to learn and explore.

Alex typing up an email to the startup, expressing his interest in joining their team. He hit 'send,' feeling a mix of excitement and anticipation for the new path he was about to embark on.

Setting:
A bustling city center, a stark contrast to Alex's quiet suburban life. The office of the blockchain startup is modern and vibrant, filled with young tech enthusiasts and visionary entrepreneurs.
Characters:
Alex: Now stepping into a more professional role in the cryptocurrency world.

Maya: Continues to be a mentor and friend, guiding Alex through new challenges.

Derek: A charismatic and visionary founder of the blockchain startup.

Elena: A seasoned developer at the startup, who becomes Alex's guide and mentor.

Narrative:
Alex's first day at the startup was a whirlwind of new faces and ideas. The office was an open space filled with enthusiastic conversations and the clatter of keyboards. He was introduced to Derek, the founder, who greeted him with a warm handshake.

"Welcome to the edge of the future, Alex," Derek said, his eyes bright with passion.

"We're not just building a product here; we're shaping a new world."

Alex, both nervous and excited, replied, "Thank you, Derek. I'm really looking forward to contributing and learning more."

As they walked through the office, Derek explained their current project - a blockchain-based platform designed to enhance supply chain transparency.

"It's about using blockchain for social good, not just finance," Derek explained. "Imagine being able to verify the ethical sourcing of your coffee or clothes with a simple app. That's what we're aiming for."

The concept immediately resonated with Alex. He remembered his conversations with Maya about the potential for blockchain to effect positive change.

Later, Alex met Elena, who would be his mentor during his time at the startup. She was a brilliant developer with a no-nonsense attitude.

"So, you're the new intern, huh?" Elena said, looking him over. "Hope you're ready to learn fast. Blockchain doesn't sleep."

Alex grinned, "I'm ready. I've been into Bitcoin for a while now."

"Bitcoin's just the tip of the iceberg, kid," Elena replied, leading him to his workstation. "Let's see how you handle the rest of the iceberg."

The days that followed were a deep dive into the world of blockchain technology. Alex was involved in various aspects of the project, from coding to market research. He found himself in a steep learning curve, absorbing everything Elena and the others taught him.

One day, during lunch, Alex sat with a group of colleagues, discussing the latest trends in cryptocurrency.

"So, Alex, you started with Bitcoin. What's your take on these new altcoins?" one colleague, Mark, asked.

Alex pondered before answering, "I think it's fascinating. Each altcoin has its own purpose, its own niche. It's not just about competing with Bitcoin anymore. It's about how each coin can innovate and solve specific problems."

"Exactly," chimed in another colleague, Priya. "It's the diversity of the ecosystem that's really exciting. There's so much potential beyond just digital currency."

These discussions were eye-opening for Alex. He began to see the broader picture of cryptocurrency and blockchain. It was not just a technological revolution; it was a cultural and economic one as well.

Alex becomes more involved in the project, contributing his insights and learning from the challenges he faces. He begins to understand the intricacies of blockchain development and its potential applications in various industries.

Chapter Two: Into the Blockchain

Setting:
A city center, inside a modern startup office.

Characters:
Alex: Now stepping into a more professional role.

Maya: Continues as a mentor and friend.

Jeff: Founder of the blockchain startup.

Elena: A developer and Alex's mentor at the startup.

Narrative:
Alex joins a blockchain startup, greeted enthusiastically by Jeff.

Jeff explains their project on enhancing supply chain transparency using blockchain.

Alex meets Elena, who becomes his mentor and introduces him to the daily operations.

Engages in discussions with colleagues about Bitcoin and the broader implications of cryptocurrencies. Learns about altcoins and the diversity of the blockchain ecosystem. Participates in project meetings and begins to contribute to coding and market research.

One afternoon, Jeff called a meeting to discuss a potential partnership with a major retail company interested in their blockchain solution.

"Team, this is a big opportunity," Jeff started, addressing the room. "Our platform could revolutionize how they track their supply chain."

Alex listened intently as Jeff outlined the proposal. He was amazed at how quickly things moved in the startup world.

After the meeting, Jeff pulled Alex aside. "I've noticed your hard work and enthusiasm. How would you feel about presenting our tech to the potential partners?"

Alex was stunned. "Really? I mean, I'd love to, but I'm not sure I'm ready."

Jeff clapped him on the shoulder. "You know more than you think, and you speak about blockchain with a genuine passion. That's what they need to see."

The days leading up to the presentation were a whirlwind of preparation. Elena helped him refine his understanding of the technical details, while Maya offered advice on public speaking.

On the day of the presentation, Alex stood before a room of corporate executives, his heart pounding. He took a deep breath and began.

"As you know, blockchain technology offers unparalleled transparency and security..." Alex started, gradually gaining confidence as he spoke.

His presentation was a success. The executives were impressed with the depth of his knowledge and the startup's innovative approach.

Afterward, Elena patted him on the back. "You nailed it, kid. You're a natural at this."

Alex begins taking on more responsibilities at the startup, diving deeper into blockchain technology, and grappling with the challenges of applying this technology in real-world scenarios.

The success of Alex's presentation marked a turning point in his time at the startup. He began to take on more challenging projects, each offering new learning opportunities and insights into the vast potential of blockchain technology.

One day, while working on integrating a new feature into their blockchain platform, Alex hit a roadblock. The code just wouldn't work as intended. Frustrated, he called Elena over.

"Elena, can you take a look at this? I can't figure out where I'm going wrong," Alex asked, rubbing his eyes.

Elena leaned over his shoulder, scanning the code on the screen. "Let's see... Ah, you need to adjust the smart contract here and here," she pointed out, her fingers darting across the screen.

"Smart contracts? I've read about them, but I've never actually worked with one," Alex admitted.

Elena sat down next to him. "Smart contracts are self-executing contracts with the terms directly written into code. They're a crucial part of many blockchain applications. Here, let me show you."

The next hour was an intense tutorial. Elena explained the nuances of smart contract development, and Alex absorbed every word. It was moments like these that made his experience at the startup invaluable.

Later in the week, Jeff announced a new initiative to explore the use of their blockchain platform in environmental conservation efforts.

"This could be a game-changer in how we track and verify carbon credits," Jeff explained excitedly during a team meeting.

Alex's interest was immediately piqued. "That's incredible. It could provide a transparent and efficient way to manage environmental projects," he chimed in.

"Exactly," Jeff agreed. "Alex, why don't you lead the preliminary research on this? You've got a knack for seeing the bigger picture."

Thrilled by the trust placed in him, Alex dove into the task. He spent days researching, talking to experts in environmental science, and exploring how blockchain could be used in this new context.

One evening, while discussing his research with Maya at a local café, he shared his excitement.

"Maya, this project could really make a difference. It's not just about technology; it's about using that technology for a meaningful cause," Alex said, his eyes alight with enthusiasm.

Maya smiled, sipping her coffee. "I told you, Alex. Blockchain has the potential to change the world in so many ways. You're right at the forefront of that change."

Alex's role at the startup becomes more pivotal. He is not only contributing to the technical aspects of the projects but also shaping their direction and purpose.
The narrative will continue to explore the challenges and breakthroughs Alex experiences, highlighting the diverse applications of blockchain technology and its impact on various industries and societal issues.

Alex's research into blockchain for environmental conservation was making significant progress. He had been reaching out to experts in the field, gathering data, and attending webinars. One afternoon, he scheduled a meeting with Jeff to discuss his findings.

In Jeff's office, Alex laid out his research. "Our platform can streamline the verification of carbon offset projects. It's about bringing transparency and efficiency to environmental efforts," he explained, pointing to his detailed report.

Jeff leaned back, impressed. "This is excellent work, Alex. It's ambitious, but it's exactly the kind of innovation we strive for."

"Thanks, Jeff. There's so much potential here. We could really make an impact," Alex replied, a sense of pride swelling in him.

As the days passed, Alex started working closely with a team dedicated to the environmental project. He found himself at the intersection of technology and sustainability, a space that was both challenging and deeply fulfilling.

One day, while working on the project, Elena approached him.

"I've been hearing great things about your work, Alex. You're really carving out a niche for yourself here," she said with a smile.

Alex felt a flush of gratitude. "I couldn't have done it without your guidance, Elena. I'm just glad to contribute to something meaningful."

"It's not just about coding or even blockchain itself," Elena said thoughtfully. "It's about the problems we can solve with it. You're seeing the bigger picture."

Their conversation was interrupted by the arrival of a new team member, Tom, who was brought in to assist with the environmental project.

"Hey, I'm Tom. Heard a lot about you, Alex," Tom greeted him with a handshake.

"Nice to meet you, Tom. Looking forward to working together," Alex replied, welcoming the new addition to the team.

As they worked together, Tom brought fresh perspectives to the project. His background in environmental science complemented Alex's technical skills, and their collaboration led to innovative ideas.

One evening, as the team stayed late to finalize a proposal, Jeff brought in pizza for everyone. They gathered around the table, taking a much-needed break.

"This feels like a start-up cliché, doesn't it? Pizza and late-night coding," Alex joked, grabbing a slice.

Jeff laughed, "It's a cliché for a reason. It's moments like these – the teamwork, the dedication – that make start-ups exciting."

As they ate, the team shared stories and insights, not just about work but about their lives and interests. It was in these moments that Alex felt a strong sense of community and purpose.

As the project advanced, Alex found himself more deeply immersed in the world of blockchain and its potential for environmental impact. He and Tom became a dynamic duo, blending technology with environmental science.

One afternoon, during a brainstorming session, Tom brought up a challenging aspect of the project. "Alex, the tech is solid, but we need to ensure that the environmental data we integrate is reliable and consistent. It's a major issue in environmental reporting."

Alex nodded, tapping his pen on his notepad. "That's a good point. Blockchain can provide transparency, but the input data needs to be credible. Maybe we can develop a protocol for data verification?"

Tom looked thoughtful. "A protocol... Yes, that could work. We'd need to collaborate with environmental agencies and experts. It would add another layer of authenticity to our platform."

Their discussion was overheard by Elena, who joined in. "You guys are onto something. But remember, the simpler we can keep the user interface, the better. We don't want to lose sight of the user experience in the complexity of the technology."

"Definitely," Alex agreed. "The challenge is to balance sophistication with simplicity."

Their conversation was a testament to the collaborative spirit of the startup. Each team member brought their expertise to the table, creating a melting pot of ideas and solutions.

Later that week, Alex presented the concept of the data verification protocol at a team meeting. The idea was met with enthusiasm, and he was tasked with leading the development of this new feature.

The following weeks were a flurry of activity. Alex liaised with environmental experts, worked on the development of the protocol, and coordinated with the rest of the team to integrate it into the platform.

During this hectic period, Maya reached out to Alex. "Hey, how's the project going? Haven't heard from you in a while."

Alex took a moment to reply, "It's been crazy busy, but good. We're working on something that could really make a difference. It's demanding, but I love the challenge."

Maya's response was encouraging. "That's great to hear, Alex. Remember, taking on challenges is how we grow. Proud of you!"
One evening, as the sun set over the city, Alex stayed late at the office, poring over lines of code. Jeff walked over to his desk.

"You're putting in a lot of hours, Alex. Make sure you're taking care of yourself too," Jeff said with a concerned tone.

Alex smiled, appreciating the concern. "Thanks, Jeff. It's just that this project... it feels important. It's more than just a job to me."
Jeff nodded, understandingly. "It's that passion that drives innovation. But even innovators need rest. Don't forget that."

Alex is balancing the demands of the project with his personal growth and well-being. The narrative explores the complexities of integrating technology with environmental sustainability, highlighting both the challenges and the breakthroughs.

The days at the startup turned into weeks, and the project on blockchain for environmental conservation grew in complexity and ambition. Alex found himself at the heart of it, coordinating between different teams and external experts.

One day, while troubleshooting a tricky aspect of the protocol integration, Alex and Elena had a thought-provoking conversation.

"Alex, I've been meaning to ask," Elena began, her eyes scanning the code on the screen, "how do you envision the future of blockchain? I mean, beyond what we're doing here."

Alex paused, considering the question. "I think blockchain has the potential to redefine not just finance or environmental conservation but governance, identity management, maybe even how we perceive trust in the digital age."

Elena nodded thoughtfully. "That's a broad vision. It's good to think big, but remember, each step we take in that direction needs to be grounded in practicality."

"You're right," Alex agreed, "but sometimes, it's the big visions that push us to innovate, to go beyond the status quo."

Their conversation was a testament to Alex's evolving perspective, a blend of idealism and pragmatism.

As the project neared its first major milestone, the team prepared for a critical review. Jeff invited a group of experts in both blockchain and environmental science to evaluate their progress.

On the day of the review, Alex felt a mixture of nerves and excitement. The conference room was filled with experts whose opinions would shape the future of their project.

"Welcome, everyone," Jeff started, "Today, we're excited to present the progress of our blockchain-based solution for environmental conservation."

Alex was up next to present the technical aspects. He took a deep breath and began, "Our platform aims to bring transparency and accountability to environmental projects. Here's how we've integrated blockchain technology to achieve that."

The presentation was interactive, with experts asking challenging questions and providing valuable feedback. Alex answered confidently, his months of hard work and immersion in the project shining through.

After the presentation, one of the experts, Dr. Hansen, a renowned environmental scientist, approached Alex. "Impressive work, young man. It's refreshing to see new technologies being applied to critical global issues."

"Thank you, Dr. Hansen," Alex replied, feeling a surge of pride.

"We believe blockchain can make a real difference in this field."

The review was a success, and the team felt a renewed sense of purpose and enthusiasm. Alex's role in this had been crucial, and he realized that he was no longer just a participant; he was a driving force in this innovative venture.

Alex continues to navigate the complexities of the project, facing both technical and ethical dilemmas. He starts to understand the delicate balance between innovation and responsibility, the importance of collaboration, and the impact of their work on real-world issues.

Chapter Three: Blockchain Horizons

Setting:
The startup's office in the bustling city center, and various locations where Alex's new responsibilities take him.

Characters:

Alex: Now more confident and influential in his role at the startup.

Elena: Continues to be a mentor and colleague, providing guidance and support.

Jeff: The founder, who begins to entrust Alex with more significant responsibilities.

Tom: Alex's colleague, focusing on the environmental aspects of the project.

New Characters:
Potential clients, partners, and other industry experts who interact with Alex and his team.

Narrative:
Chapter Three opens with Alex preparing for a significant industry conference, where he is set to speak about their project's latest advancements.

A few days before the conference, Alex and Elena are working late, fine-tuning the presentation.

Elena looks over the slides and says, "You've got the technical details down, Alex. But remember, your audience isn't just techies. You need to make it relatable to everyone there."

Alex nods, taking in her advice. "You're right. I'll add some real-world examples, make it more tangible."

The night before the conference, Alex is at home, practicing his speech. His mother pops her head in his room, "You're going to do great, Alex. Just speak from your heart."

Alex smiles, "Thanks, Mom. It's a big opportunity to showcase our work."

The conference day arrives. Alex stands backstage, going over his notes one last time. Jeff joins him, giving him an encouraging pat on the back. "You've got this, Alex. Show them what we've achieved."

On stage, Alex starts his presentation. "Good morning, everyone. Today, I'm excited to share how our blockchain platform is not just a technological innovation but a tool for positive environmental change."

The audience listens intently as Alex articulates the vision and capabilities of their project, using clear examples to highlight its impact.

After the presentation, a number of attendees approach Alex, expressing interest in their project and asking detailed questions. Among them is a representative from a large non-profit organization, Ms. Anderson.

"That was an inspiring presentation, Mr. Alex. Our organization has been looking for a solution like yours. Could we set up a meeting to discuss a potential collaboration?" Ms. Anderson inquires.

Alex is thrilled, "Absolutely, Ms. Anderson. I'll coordinate with our team and set something up."

Back at the office, the team congratulates Alex on his successful presentation. Jeff discusses the potential collaboration with the non-profit.

"This could be a major partnership, Alex. I want you to lead the discussions with Ms. Anderson's team," Jeff says, entrusting him with the responsibility.

Alex is now taking a more front-facing role in the startup. He engages in meetings with Ms. Anderson and her team, navigating the intricacies of forming a partnership that aligns with both their project goals and the non-profit's mission.

Alex faces the complexities of business negotiations, the challenge of aligning technological possibilities with real-world needs, and the importance of maintaining the startup's vision and values in potential partnerships.

Back at the startup, Alex's newfound confidence and exposure begin to reflect in his day-to-day work. He becomes more involved in strategic decision-making, often consulting with Jeff and the senior team on the direction of their project.

During one strategy meeting, Jeff poses a challenging question to the team. "We've made great strides with our platform, but how do we ensure scalability and adaptability as blockchain technology evolves?"

Alex, deep in thought, responds, "One approach could be modular design—building our platform in such a way that it can easily adapt to changes and integrate new advancements in blockchain technology."

Jeff nods appreciatively. "Good thinking, Alex. Let's explore that route further."

The conversation underscores the dynamic nature of the blockchain industry and the need for continuous innovation and adaptability.

As the partnership with the non-profit organization solidifies, Alex is tasked with overseeing the integration of their platform with the organization's systems. He collaborates closely with Tom and a team of developers, ensuring a seamless and secure implementation.

During one of the integration sessions, Tom remarks, "Alex, you've really taken the lead on this. It's impressive how you've managed to bridge the gap between tech and real-world application."

Alex smiles, acknowledging the compliment. "Thanks, Tom. It's been a team effort, though. We're making something meaningful here."

However, with new responsibilities come new challenges. Alex finds himself juggling multiple aspects of the project, from technical development to client relations and team management. The pressure mounts, and he starts to feel the strain.

One evening, feeling particularly overwhelmed, Alex confides in Maya over a phone call. "It's a lot, Maya. Sometimes I wonder if I've taken on too much."

Maya listens sympathetically, then offers advice. "Alex, it's okay to feel overwhelmed. What you're doing isn't easy. But remember, it's important to step back sometimes, to look at the bigger picture. Take a break if you need to. The work will still be there when you return."

Her words resonate with Alex, reminding him of the importance of balance and self-care.

Following Maya's advice, Alex takes a short break, stepping away from the hectic pace of the startup. He spends time with his family, revisits old hobbies, and reflects on his journey. The break proves to be rejuvenating, and he returns to work with renewed energy and clarity.

Alex's perspectives on leadership, innovation, and the ethical dimensions of technology continue to evolve. He writes a thought-provoking article on the future of blockchain, which gets published in a prominent tech magazine, further establishing him as a voice in the industry.

Chapter Four: Pooling Resources

Setting:
Transitioning from the startup's office to the broader Bitcoin mining community, including online forums and collaborative spaces.

Characters:
Alex: Continuing his journey in the Bitcoin world.

Elena: Provides technical support and guidance.

Tom: Engages in the mining pool decision.

New Characters: Members of the mining pool community.

Narrative:
Alex, Elena, and Tom discussing the increasing difficulty of mining Bitcoin due to competition from larger, more equipped miners.

Elena addresses the team, "The mining landscape is changing. Individual mining isn't as viable as it used to be. It's time we consider joining a mining pool."

Alex nods in agreement, "A mining pool could increase our chances of earning Bitcoin. Instead of going at it alone, we combine our resources with others."

Tom, looking intrigued, asks, "But how does that work exactly? How do we ensure fairness in a pool?"

Alex explains, "In a mining pool, each member contributes their computing power. When the pool successfully mines a block, the reward is distributed among members, proportionate to their contribution."

The team decides to research different mining pools, evaluating their size, fee structure, and reputation within the community.

In their search, they come across a well-regarded pool known for its transparency and community support. Alex reaches out to the pool's administrator, a seasoned miner named Dave.

During a video call, Dave explains further, "Our pool is about more than just mining; it's a community. We share knowledge, support each other, and work together to improve our mining efficiency."

Alex, impressed with Dave's ethos, discusses with the team, and they agree to join the pool. They reconfigure their mining setups to contribute to the pool's collective efforts.

As they start mining in the pool, they notice a significant improvement in their mining returns. The decision to pool resources pays off, validating their strategic shift.

One evening, in an online meeting with the pool community, a member raises a concern, "With the increasing energy consumption of Bitcoin mining, are we contributing to environmental issues?"

The question sparks a thoughtful discussion. Alex contributes, "It's a valid concern. We need to think about sustainable mining practices. Maybe there's a way to offset our carbon footprint."

The dialogue leads to the pool collectively deciding to invest in renewable energy sources, demonstrating the pool's commitment not just to mining but to responsible and sustainable practices.

Alex, Elena, and Tom navigate the complexities of being part of a mining pool. They learn about the importance of collaboration, the nuances of trust and transparency in pooled efforts, and the collective responsibility of miners.

In the weeks following their decision to join the mining pool, Alex, Elena, and Tom engage more actively with the pool's community. They participate in regular virtual meetings, discussing strategies and sharing insights on Bitcoin mining.

During one of these meetings, a newer member of the pool, Jasmine, expresses frustration. "I've been contributing my computing power, but it feels like I'm not earning as much as I should.

How is the reward distribution really calculated?" Alex jumps in to explain, "The rewards are proportional to the amount of work each miner contributes. It's all about the hash rate you bring to the pool. Higher hash rate, higher share of the reward."

Jasmine nods, understanding dawning. "So, it's in my interest to optimize my mining setup. Got it." Elena adds, "And it's not just about individual earnings. Being in this pool is a collective effort. We succeed together."

As the conversation continues, Tom brings up a new topic. "I've been reading about the latest developments in Bitcoin mining technology. There are more energy-efficient machines now. Should we consider upgrading?"

The team deliberates on this, weighing the costs against the potential increase in mining efficiency. They decide to present this idea to the pool community, suggesting a collective investment in more sustainable mining technology.

Dave, the pool administrator, appreciates the initiative. "This is what I love about our community. You're thinking ahead, not just for yourselves but for the pool as a whole. Let's put this to a vote."

The proposal is met with enthusiasm, and the pool members agree to invest in upgrading their mining equipment. This decision marks a significant step for the pool, moving towards more sustainable and efficient mining practices.

In the following weeks, Alex takes on a more prominent role in the pool, often leading discussions and helping less experienced members optimize their mining setups. His expertise and willingness to help others do not go unnoticed.

One evening, during a casual chat session within the pool, an older member, Greg, comments, "Alex, you've really become a pillar of this community. Your knowledge and your approach to teamwork are impressive."

Alex feels a sense of accomplishment. "Thanks, Greg. I've learned so much from all of you. It's great to be part of a community that's not just about profit but about supporting each other."

The narrative explores the evolving dynamics within the mining pool. Alex and his team face new challenges, such as fluctuations in Bitcoin's value and changes in the global mining landscape. They navigate these challenges by leaning on the collective wisdom and support of the pool community.

Through these experiences, Alex gains a deeper understanding of the importance of collaboration and community in the world of Bitcoin mining. He starts to see the mining pool not just as a means to earn Bitcoin but as a microcosm of the larger Bitcoin ecosystem, where cooperation, trust, and shared goals are key to success.

As the mining pool adapts to the new, more efficient mining equipment, Alex begins to notice a shift in the dynamics of the pool. The increased efficiency leads to higher expectations, and some members start to push for more aggressive strategies to maximize profits.

During a heated discussion in an online meeting, a member named Carl argues, "We need to focus on maximizing our earnings. With the new equipment, we should be aiming to dominate more of the mining network."

Alex, however, senses the potential risks of such an approach. "While it's important to be competitive, we shouldn't lose sight of our initial ethos. This pool is about collaboration and sustainable practices, not just dominating the network."

Elena supports Alex's standpoint. "Alex is right. There's a balance to be struck. We need to ensure that our strategies don't compromise the integrity of the pool or the wider Bitcoin community."

The debate intensifies, with members divided on the pool's direction. Alex realizes the importance of maintaining a unified vision and the challenges of leading a diverse group with varying motivations.

In an effort to mediate the situation, Alex proposes a compromise. "Let's set up a committee to explore various strategies, focusing on both profitability and sustainability. We can then make informed decisions based on their findings."

The idea is well-received, and a committee is formed, with Alex as one of the key members. This role places him at the forefront of decision-making in the pool, giving him a new perspective on leadership and responsibility.

As the committee conducts its research, Alex spends time analyzing market trends, technological advancements, and the environmental impact of mining. He engages with experts outside the pool, broadening his understanding of the global landscape of Bitcoin mining.

One evening, while discussing the committee's progress with Tom, Alex shares his insights. "The world of Bitcoin mining is more complex than I realized. It's not just about hash rates and profits. There's a whole ecosystem out there, and our decisions here can have wider implications."

Tom nods, "It's a lot of responsibility. But I think we're up for the challenge. We're not just miners; we're part of a community that's shaping the future of Bitcoin."

Their discussion is a moment of reflection for Alex, acknowledging the weight of his responsibilities and the impact of their collective actions.

The narrative delves into the committee's findings and the decisions made by the pool. Through these developments, Alex confronts the realities of leadership, the importance of ethical decision-making in business, and the challenges of balancing diverse viewpoints within a community.

As the committee's work progresses, Alex finds himself often in discussions with members who hold differing views on the future of the mining pool. One day, he has a particularly challenging conversation with a member named Rachel, who is vocal about aggressive expansion.

Rachel argues during an online meeting, "We need to push harder. With our current resources, we could easily increase our control over the mining network and boost our profits significantly."

Alex, understanding her perspective, responds calmly, "I hear your point, Rachel, but we have to consider the long-term impact of such actions. Aggressive expansion could lead to centralization, which goes against the very principle of Bitcoin."

The discussion goes back and forth, with Alex advocating for a more measured approach that balances profitability with the ethics of decentralization. The conversation reflects the broader debate within the Bitcoin community about growth versus sustainability.

Later, Alex seeks advice from Elena, who has become a trusted mentor. "Elena, how do you handle situations where there's a clear divide in opinion? It's tough to find a middle ground."

Elena offers her perspective, "In a community like ours, it's about finding consensus. It's not always easy, but it's important to listen and try to understand different viewpoints. Ultimately, our decisions should reflect the collective best interest."

Her words resonate with Alex, reinforcing the importance of collaborative decision-making in a diverse community.

In the meantime, Tom works on developing a model to assess the environmental impact of their mining activities. He presents his findings to the pool, highlighting ways to reduce their carbon footprint.

"Based on my analysis, if we invest in renewable energy sources for our mining operations, we can significantly reduce our environmental impact," Tom explains during a virtual meeting.

This proposal sparks interest among many members, aligning with the pool's commitment to sustainable practices. The pool votes in favor of investing in renewable energy, a decision that is well-received by the wider community and enhances the pool's reputation.

The narrative focuses on the implementation of the renewable energy initiative and the ongoing efforts to balance growth with ethical practices. Alex, now recognized as a key figure in the pool, continues to navigate the complexities of leadership, advocating for responsible and sustainable mining practices.

One evening, in a reflective conversation with Maya, Alex shares his thoughts. "It's been a journey, Maya. Managing these diverse perspectives and leading responsibly – it's challenging but rewarding."

Maya replies, "You're doing great, Alex. It's about making a positive impact, and you're certainly doing that. Keep steering the course."

The decision to invest in renewable energy sources marks a significant achievement for the mining pool. The members, inspired by the leadership and vision of Alex and his team, begin to see the tangible effects of their collective decisions.

In a virtual celebration of the pool's latest milestone, Alex addresses the members. "Thanks to everyone's effort and commitment, we're not just mining Bitcoin; we're setting an example for responsible and sustainable practices in the cryptocurrency world."

His speech is met with virtual applause and words of encouragement from the members, solidifying the sense of community and shared purpose within the pool.

Alex reflects on the journey so far. He realizes that the lessons learned and the challenges overcome have prepared him for the next phase of his adventure in the world of Bitcoin and blockchain.

One evening, while discussing future plans with Elena and Tom, Alex brings up a new idea. "I've been thinking about how we can further leverage our experience and knowledge. What if we start consulting for other pools and organizations looking to implement sustainable mining practices?"

Elena looks intrigued. "That's a great idea, Alex. There's a growing interest in sustainable practices in the crypto community. We could really make an impact."

Tom adds, "And it's not just about sustainability. We've learned so much about community building, decision-making, and balancing growth with ethics. There's a lot we can offer."

Encouraged by their enthusiasm, Alex decides to pursue this new venture. They start outlining a plan to offer consulting services, leveraging their expertise and experience.

As they brainstorm, Alex receives a message from Jeff, who has been following their progress closely. "I heard about your new initiative. Let's meet up. I think there's potential for collaboration with the startup."

This message marks a turning point, signaling the beginning of a new chapter in Alex's journey. The narrative begins to transition, hinting at broader horizons and new opportunities that lie ahead.

The final scenes show Alex, Elena, and Tom in a meeting with Jeff, discussing possibilities of integrating their new venture with the startup's expanding portfolio.

Jeff proposes, "Your expertise in sustainable mining practices is invaluable. It aligns perfectly with our vision. Let's explore how we can work together to bring this to a wider audience."

Alex is feeling a sense of accomplishment and anticipation. The experiences in the mining pool have not only contributed to his personal and professional growth but are also opening new doors and possibilities.

Moving forward to Chapter Five of "Byte Rich: The Bitcoin Odyssey," the focus shifts to a blockchain conference where Alex and his team engage with pioneers in the field, offering a platform to explore the vast applications of blockchain technology.

Chapter Five: Blockchain Pioneers

Setting:
A major blockchain conference held in a large metropolitan city, bustling with innovators, entrepreneurs, and experts from various sectors.

Characters:
Alex: Continues to grow as a blockchain enthusiast and professional.

Elena and Tom: Join Alex at the conference, bringing their unique perspectives.

New Characters: Various pioneers and experts in the field of blockchain technology.

Narrative:
Alex, Elena, and Tom arrive at the blockchain conference, a hub of innovation and discussion. The atmosphere is electric with the energy of like-minded individuals all passionate about the potential of blockchain technology.

Walking through the conference hall, Elena remarks, "This is incredible, Alex. The diversity of applications for blockchain being showcased here is mind-blowing."

Alex nods in agreement, "It's not just about cryptocurrencies anymore. It's about how blockchain can revolutionize various industries."

Their first stop is a panel discussion titled "Blockchain in Healthcare." The panelists, including medical professionals and tech innovators, discuss how blockchain can enhance patient data security and improve the efficiency of medical supply chains.

Tom, intrigued, leans over to Alex and whispers, "The potential for blockchain in healthcare is massive. Imagine the implications for patient privacy and global health initiatives."

As they move between sessions, Alex's attention is drawn to a workshop on "Blockchain and Environmental Sustainability." The workshop leader, Dr. Lisa Park, demonstrates how blockchain technology is being used to track carbon footprints and support renewable energy initiatives.

Alex engages in a discussion with Dr. Park after the workshop. "Dr. Park, your work is inspiring. I've been involved in a project that focuses on sustainable Bitcoin mining. Your insights could be incredibly valuable to us."

Dr. Park responds with interest, "Sustainable mining, you say? That's a crucial area. I'd love to learn more and explore potential collaborations."

Throughout the day, the team attends various other sessions, including ones on blockchain in finance, governance, and supply chain management. Each session opens their eyes to new possibilities and applications of blockchain technology.

In the evening, at a networking event, Alex, Elena, and Tom find themselves in conversation with a group of entrepreneurs who are working on a blockchain-based voting system.

One of the entrepreneurs, Max, shares his vision, "Imagine a world where voting is completely transparent, secure, and accessible from your own device. Blockchain can make that a reality."

Tom is visibly excited by the idea. "That would revolutionize our democratic processes. The transparency and security of blockchain could restore trust in our electoral systems."

The conference serves as a catalyst for Alex and his team, inspiring them with new ideas and potential projects. They leave each day of the conference energized and full of thoughts on how to integrate these new learnings into their work.

The narrative explores how Alex and his team begin to envision new projects inspired by the conference. They start to plan how they can contribute to these groundbreaking applications of blockchain technology, broadening their scope beyond just Bitcoin and cryptocurrency.

The second day of the conference brings even more opportunities for learning and networking. Alex, Elena, and Tom start their day at a session titled "Decentralized Finance (DeFi): The Future of Banking."

As the speaker delves into how blockchain is reshaping financial services, offering more inclusive and transparent systems, Alex turns to Elena and says, "DeFi could be the key to unlocking financial services for unbanked populations around the world."

Elena nods in agreement, "It's a revolution in finance. The implications are enormous, especially in terms of accessibility and equality."

Later, at a panel discussion about "Blockchain for Social Good," they listen to representatives from various non-profits discuss how blockchain can be used to enhance transparency in charitable organizations and increase the impact of social projects.

Tom, moved by the discussions, shares his thoughts with the team. "It's incredible how blockchain can be a force for good, addressing real-world issues like poverty and inequality."

During a break, Alex has a chance encounter with a pioneer in the field of blockchain, Dr. Anita Roy, known for her work in digital identity verification.

Alex introduces himself, "Dr. Roy, I'm Alex. I've been following your work on digital identity. It's fascinating how blockchain can empower individuals with control over their personal data."

Dr. Roy smiles warmly, "Thank you, Alex. Yes, blockchain has the potential to revolutionize identity management, making it more secure and user-centric. Are you working on something in this area?"

Alex shakes his head, "Not currently, but it's an area we're interested in exploring."

Dr. Roy hands him her business card. "Let's stay in touch. Collaborations often lead to wonderful innovations."

The day concludes with a keynote speech about the future of blockchain technology. The speaker, a renowned technologist, paints a picture of a world interconnected and empowered by blockchain.

As they leave the conference hall, Elena reflects, "This conference has been an eye-opener. The potential applications of blockchain are almost limitless."

Tom adds enthusiastically, "We're at the forefront of something huge. I can't wait to see where we take this next."

On their last night at the conference, Alex, Elena, and Tom gather for dinner, discussing the myriad ways they could incorporate their newfound knowledge into their work.

Alex proposes, "Why don't we hold a brainstorming session when we get back? We could explore new projects, especially in areas like DeFi and digital identity."

Elena agrees, "That's a great idea. And let's involve the rest of the team. Fresh perspectives can spark brilliant ideas."

As the evening draws to a close, the narrative sets the stage for Alex and his team to embark on new ventures, inspired by the groundbreaking ideas and pioneers they encountered at the conference. Their conversations and plans hint at exciting developments to come, showcasing their commitment to leveraging blockchain technology for innovative and socially impactful projects.

Back at the startup, the energy from the conference is still palpable. Alex, Elena, and Tom organize a brainstorming session with the rest of the team to discuss potential new projects inspired by the conference.

Gathering in the conference room, Alex starts the meeting with enthusiasm. "The blockchain conference opened our eyes to so many possibilities. Let's use this session to brainstorm how we can apply what we learned to new projects."

Elena, always pragmatic, adds, "Remember, we need to think about feasibility and how these projects align with our startup's mission and resources."

One of the team members, Sarah, who has been researching blockchain in supply chain management, pitches an idea. "What about a blockchain solution for supply chain transparency? It could help companies track the ethical sourcing of their products."

Tom, excited by the idea, chimes in, "That aligns perfectly with our focus on sustainability. We could even integrate it with environmental tracking to add more value."

The team discusses the idea further, considering the technical requirements and potential market for such a solution. Alex takes notes, visibly excited about the potential of this new project.

Later, Alex has a call with Dr. Roy, discussing potential collaboration on a digital identity project. Dr. Roy shares valuable insights, "Digital identity is about giving control back to the users.

Blockchain can provide a secure and decentralized way of managing identities."
Alex replies, "That's exactly what we're interested in exploring. There's so much potential

for impact, especially in areas where identity verification is a barrier to accessing services."

The conversation with Dr. Roy sparks further ideas about how the startup could venture into the realm of digital identity, possibly creating solutions for underprivileged communities who lack formal identification.

Alex, Elena, and Tom work on developing proposals for these new projects. They engage in deep research, talk to experts, and start sketching out potential models.

During one late-night working session, Elena looks up from her laptop and says, "You know, Alex, it's amazing how far we've come. From mining Bitcoin to potentially changing how people access services and verify their identity."

Alex nods, feeling a sense of pride and responsibility. "It's a big leap, but I think we're ready for it. We're not just tech enthusiasts anymore; we're pioneers in our own right."

The team submitting proposals for the new projects. Alex feels a mix of anticipation and determination. He knows that they are stepping into new territory, but he's confident in the team's ability to innovate and make a difference.

With the proposals for new projects submitted, the team waits anxiously for feedback. A few days later, Jeff calls a meeting to discuss the way forward.

In the meeting, Jeff addresses the team, "I've reviewed your proposals, and I must say, I'm impressed. These projects could really put us on the map as innovators in the blockchain space.

Let's greenlight the supply chain transparency project and the digital identity initiative."
The team erupts in cheers, excited to embark on these new ventures. Alex feels a surge of pride and responsibility, knowing that their ideas will now come to life.

As they start working on the projects, they encounter various challenges. The supply chain project requires intricate understanding of global trade processes, and the digital identity initiative poses complex privacy and security considerations.

One afternoon, while troubleshooting an issue with the digital identity model, Tom expresses his concerns to Alex. "This is more complicated than I thought. Ensuring privacy while maintaining a decentralized system is a tough balance."

Alex, focused on finding a solution, replies, "It's a challenge, but it's also what makes this project important. We're treading new ground here, and we have to be innovative in our approach."

Their conversation is interrupted by a call from Sarah, who's been leading the research for the supply chain project. "Guys, I've got some interesting insights from a potential partner in the fashion industry. They're keen on using our platform to showcase their ethical sourcing practices."

This news brings a new wave of enthusiasm to the team. They realize the real-world impact their work could have, driving them to overcome the technical hurdles.

In the following weeks, Alex finds himself juggling between the two projects, coordinating with team members, and liaising with potential partners and experts. The workload is immense, but his passion for the work keeps him going.

During a late-night work session, Elena looks at Alex, "You know, despite the challenges, it's projects like these that remind me why I got into blockchain in the first place."

Alex nods in agreement, "It's about making a difference, right? Using technology to solve real problems."

The narrative focuses on the progress of the projects. The supply chain transparency project begins a pilot phase with the fashion industry partner, and the digital identity initiative starts gaining attention for its innovative approach to privacy and security.

One evening, reflecting on the day's work, Alex shares his thoughts with the team. "We're not just building solutions; we're building the future. It's hard work, but it's worth it."

The day closes with the team preparing for a major presentation to showcase their progress to investors and industry leaders. The anticipation and excitement are palpable, setting the stage for new developments and opportunities in the chapters to come.

As we continue with Chapter Five of "Byte Rich: The Bitcoin Odyssey," we prepare for the transition to Chapter Six, focusing on the culmination of the team's efforts and the anticipation of new beginnings.

The day of the major presentation has arrived. The startup's office is buzzing with activity as the team makes final preparations. Alex, Elena, and Tom review their slides, each feeling a mix of nerves and excitement.

Elena turns to Alex, "This presentation is more than just an update. It's a showcase of our vision and capabilities. We've really pushed the boundaries with these projects."

Tom, looking over the digital identity project slides, adds, "We're not just tech developers anymore; we're innovators solving real-world problems. It's a big moment for us."

Alex nods in agreement, feeling the weight of the occasion. "Let's make sure we communicate our passion and the potential impact of these projects. This is just the beginning."

As they arrive at the venue, they are greeted by a room full of investors, industry experts, and media representatives. The atmosphere is charged with anticipation.

Jeff introduces the team, "Today, you'll see how our startup is leading the way in utilizing blockchain for meaningful and impactful solutions."

Alex starts the presentation with the supply chain transparency project. "Our platform uses blockchain to bring unprecedented transparency to supply chains, ensuring ethical practices and sustainability."

The audience listens intently as Alex, Elena, and Tom take turns explaining the technical aspects, the pilot project with the fashion industry partner, and the potential global impact.

Moving on to the digital identity initiative, Tom takes the lead. "Our digital identity solution is about empowerment and security. It gives control back to individuals over their personal data."

The presentation is well-received, with several attendees approaching the team afterward with questions and potential collaboration ideas.

As the event winds down, Jeff pulls Alex aside. "That was outstanding. I think it's time we discuss taking these projects to the next level. Let's talk tomorrow about expansion plans."

Alex feels a surge of accomplishment and anticipation for the future. He realizes that the journey they embarked on is evolving, leading them to new challenges and opportunities.

The final scenes of Chapter Five show the team celebrating their successful presentation. They reflect on their journey, the challenges they've overcome, and the path ahead.

Alex shares his thoughts with the team, "This is just the start. We've laid a strong foundation, and now we're ready to build on it. Chapter Six of our journey is about scaling these projects and exploring new horizons."

The team is looking ahead, ready to embrace the next phase of their adventure in the blockchain world, signaling the transition to Chapter Six.

Beginning Chapter Six of "Byte Rich: The Bitcoin Odyssey," we explore the implications of a sudden spike in Bitcoin's value, focusing on how this newfound wealth affects Alex and his team, and the challenges and ethical considerations they face.

Chapter Six: Byte Rich, Byte Wise

Setting:
The startup's office and various personal settings that reflect the trio's changing circumstances due to their increased wealth.

Characters:
Alex: Faces the complexities of newfound wealth and its responsibilities.

Elena and Tom: Also navigate the changes and challenges brought on by their financial success.

Jeff: Provides guidance and perspective on managing wealth and business growth.

New Characters: Financial advisors, family members, and others affected by the trio's wealth.

Narrative:
Alex, Elena, and Tom are seen in a meeting with Jeff, discussing the unexpected surge in Bitcoin's value. Their early investments and the success of their projects have significantly increased their wealth.

Jeff, with years of experience, advises, "This windfall is both an opportunity and a responsibility. How you manage this wealth will define not just your futures, but also the impact you can have."

Alex, feeling a mix of excitement and uncertainty, shares his thoughts with Elena and Tom later. "This changes everything. We need to think about how we use this wealth. It's not just about us; it's about how we can contribute to the community." Elena, always pragmatic, suggests, "We should consult with financial experts. We need a strategy to manage our funds wisely."

The trio decides to meet with a financial advisor, who provides insights into wealth management, investment strategies, and the importance of diversification.

During a discussion at Tom's apartment, the conversation shifts to the ethical aspects of their wealth. Tom expresses his concern, "We've seen how money can change people. I don't want us to lose sight of who we are and why we started this journey."

Alex nods in agreement, "Our ethics have always guided us. This money won't change that. In fact, it gives us the resources to make even more of a positive impact."

The narrative then explores how each member of the trio uses their wealth. Alex decides to set up a scholarship fund for aspiring blockchain developers, Elena invests in tech startups focusing on social issues, and Tom donates to environmental causes, staying true to their values and the mission of their startup.

The trio also faces the challenges that come with wealth. They deal with increased attention, both positive and negative, and the complexities of balancing personal life with their professional ambitions.

One evening, while having dinner with his family, Alex faces questions from his relatives about his sudden wealth. His mother, concerned, says, "Alex, we're proud of you, but remember that money isn't everything. Stay true to yourself." Alex reassures her, "Don't worry, Mom. I won't let this change me. I want to use this opportunity to do more good."

The day continues with the trio navigating their new reality, making decisions about investments, philanthropy, and the future of their startup.

They learn valuable lessons about financial wisdom, the responsibilities that come with wealth, and the importance of staying grounded despite their success.

As the trio continues to adjust to their newfound wealth, they face various situations that test their values and decision-making. One day, Alex and Elena have a meeting with a group of investors interested in their startup.

During the meeting, one investor, Mr. Hamilton, makes a proposal. "Your startup has great potential. We're willing to invest significantly, but we'd like to see a shift in focus. More profit-driven projects."

Alex exchanges a glance with Elena. He responds carefully, "We appreciate the offer, Mr. Hamilton, but our mission has always been to use blockchain for positive social impact. We're not willing to compromise on that."

Elena adds, "Our projects have a broader aim than just profit. We believe in creating value that benefits society as a whole."

The investor nods, albeit slightly disappointed. "I respect your stance. Let's see if there are other areas where our interests align."

After the investors leave, Alex and Elena discuss the importance of staying true to their vision, even in the face of tempting offers.

Meanwhile, Tom grapples with his personal life being impacted by his new wealth. During a visit to his hometown, he finds his old friends treating him differently, some with admiration, others with envy.

Tom shares his feelings with Alex over a coffee. "It's like they see me as a different person now. I just want to be the same old Tom to them."

Alex empathizes, "Wealth can change dynamics, unfortunately. But the people who truly matter will see you for who you are, not what you have." In another development, the trio decides to use part of their wealth to launch a community initiative focusing on educating underprivileged youth about technology and blockchain. They discuss plans to set up workshops and provide resources to local schools.

Elena, excited about the initiative, says, "This is exactly the kind of impact we should be making. Empowering the next generation with knowledge and skills."

They face the complexities of managing their personal relationships in light of their wealth. They also navigate the responsibilities of being public figures in the blockchain community, often speaking at events and participating in discussions about the ethical use of technology and wealth.

One evening, at a community event, Alex speaks to a group of young enthusiasts. "Success in technology or any field isn't just about what you achieve for yourself. It's about how you use your success to lift others up and drive positive change."

The trio was reflecting on their journey. They have grown not just in terms of wealth but also in their understanding of the impact they can have.

They reaffirm their commitment to using their resources and influence for the greater good, setting the stage for new challenges and adventures.

As the trio continues to grapple with their changed circumstances, they decide to have a meeting to discuss the long-term vision for their wealth and the startup.

In the meeting, Alex starts, "We've been given a rare opportunity. This wealth can enable us to pursue projects we've only dreamed of. But we need a clear plan."

Elena, who has been thinking deeply about this, suggests, "We should allocate a portion of our wealth to fund research and development in emerging blockchain technologies. Innovation should remain our cornerstone."

Tom adds, "And let's not forget about giving back. Part of our funds should go to social causes, especially in education and environmental conservation."

The discussion leads to a comprehensive plan where they allocate funds for innovation, social projects, personal investments, and expanding the startup.

Meanwhile, the impact of their success on their personal lives continues to unfold. Elena finds herself the subject of media attention, which she struggles to handle. She confides in Alex during a quiet moment at the office.

"I never expected this level of attention. It's overwhelming, and honestly, a bit invasive," Elena shares, looking troubled.

Alex nods sympathetically, "It's a side effect of success we didn't anticipate. But remember, you have the right to your privacy. We can work with a PR team to manage this."

Elena appreciates the support, "Thanks, Alex. It's good to know I'm not alone in this."

As the day progresses, Tom takes a proactive step in addressing the environmental impact of blockchain technology. He organizes a seminar inviting experts to discuss sustainable practices in the industry. The event is well-attended, signaling the growing concern and interest in the topic.

After the seminar, Tom reflects, "There's so much potential to use our resources for good. Today was just the start. We can lead the way in making blockchain more environmentally friendly."

Their newfound wealth also allows Alex to reconnect with his family on a deeper level. He takes his parents on a trip, where they have heartfelt conversations about his journey, his success, and how it has changed their family.

His father, in a moment of quiet reflection, tells Alex, "Son, we're proud of you, not just for what you've achieved, but for who you've become. Stay grounded and true to yourself."

As the day comes to a close, the trio sits together, looking out at the city skyline. They talk about the future, their dreams, and the legacy they want to leave. The conversation is filled with hope, ambition, and a sense of responsibility.

Alex finally says, "We've come a long way, but our journey is far from over. We have the means to make a real difference now. Let's ensure we use it wisely and for the betterment of society."

The team nears its summary conclusion, Alex, Elena, and Tom are seen reflecting on their recent successes and the changes in their lives. They recognize that with their newfound wealth and influence comes a responsibility to pave the way for future innovations and ethical practices in the blockchain space.

In a quiet moment at the office, Tom brings up a new concern. "With all this attention on us now, I think we need to be even more mindful of how we present ourselves and our projects. Our actions are under scrutiny."

Elena agrees, "You're right, Tom. We've become role models in a way. It's important that we lead by example, especially as we plan for our next big venture."

Alex, feeling the weight of their words, adds, "Our next chapter is about setting new standards in the industry. We've made an impact locally, but now it's time to think bigger, to have a global influence."

The trio begins to outline plans for an international conference hosted by their startup, aiming to bring together leading minds in blockchain and discuss the future of the technology. The conference would also serve as a platform to launch their new projects and initiatives.

As they discuss the details, Jeff joins them, offering his insights. "This conference could be a landmark event. It's an opportunity to showcase our advancements and set the agenda for ethical and sustainable blockchain development."

The planning for the conference takes on a life of its own, with the trio working tirelessly to line up speakers, secure sponsorships, and create an agenda that reflects their vision for the future of blockchain.

In one planning session, Alex says, "We want this conference to be a turning point. Let's focus on themes like accessibility, sustainability, and the social impact of blockchain."

Elena, looking over the list of potential speakers, suggests, "We should also include voices that are often underrepresented in tech. Diversity in perspective is crucial."

As they finalize the preparations for the conference, the narrative begins to transition towards Chapter Seven. The trio's excitement and anticipation for the event are palpable.

The team standing in the soon-to-be-filled conference hall, looking over the empty seats that will soon host guests from around the world. Tom, looking around, says, "Can you believe how far we've come? This conference is just the beginning of our next chapter."

Alex responds, "We're shaping the future, one byte at a time. Let's make this a memorable one."

Chapter Seven: Scaling New Heights

Setting:
The startup's office, various meeting rooms, and government offices for regulatory discussions.

Characters:
Alex: Now a seasoned entrepreneur facing new challenges.

Elena and Tom: Continue to support and contribute to the expanding operations.

Jeff: Provides mentorship and guidance through the expansion.

New Characters: Government officials, regulatory experts, and additional team members hired to support the expansion.

Narrative:
Alex, Elena, and Tom in a strategy meeting, discussing the expansion of their startup. The room is filled with charts, graphs, and various business plans.

Alex addresses the team, "Expanding our operation means we'll face new challenges, especially in terms of technology and compliance. We need to be prepared for that."

Elena, looking at the technical roadmap, adds, "Our tech infrastructure needs to be scalable. We have to anticipate growing user numbers and data volume."

Tom, focusing on the regulatory aspect, mentions, "And let's not forget the legal side of things. With different countries having varied regulations on blockchain and cryptocurrencies, we need to navigate this carefully."

The conversation shifts to the need for hiring additional talent to support their growth. They discuss creating new departments and the importance of maintaining their company culture during this expansion.

As they proceed with their expansion plans, the trio encounters their first major hurdle: a regulatory challenge. A new government policy on cryptocurrency is introduced, complicating their operations. They arrange a meeting with a regulatory expert, Ms. Parker, to seek advice.

In the meeting, Ms. Parker explains, "The new regulations require stricter compliance in areas like user verification and transaction monitoring. You'll need to adjust your operations to adhere to these."

Alex, concerned, replies, "We understand the importance of compliance, but these regulations could slow down our processes. We need to find a balance."

The narrative then follows the team as they work to align their operations with the new regulations while trying to maintain efficiency and user experience.

During a team meeting, Elena raises a crucial point, "As we expand, we should also focus on user education. With new regulations and technologies, it's important our users understand how to navigate this space safely."

Tom adds, "And let's make sure we're transparent with our users about how these changes affect them. Trust is key in our business."

The day progresses with the team overcoming these initial regulatory challenges, adapting their business model, and implementing new systems to ensure compliance. They also launch a series of educational initiatives to help their users understand the evolving landscape of cryptocurrency.

In a reflective moment, Alex discusses with Jeff the journey so far. "Expanding hasn't been easy, but it's necessary. We're not just building a business; we're contributing to the shaping of an industry."

Jeff nods, offering his insight, "Growth is always challenging, but it's also rewarding. You're learning what it truly means to be entrepreneurs in a rapidly changing world."

As evening nears its end, the narrative begins to transition towards new developments. The team prepares for the official launch of their expanded operation, planning a significant event to mark the occasion.

The final scene of the chapter shows the team in a moment of calm before the storm, aware of the challenges ahead but ready to face them head-on.

Alex shares his final thoughts before the chapter closes, "We've scaled new heights, faced hurdles, and adapted. Now, it's time to take the next step. Let's show the world what we're capable of."

As the date of the official launch of their expanded operation approaches, the team works tirelessly to ensure everything is in place. They encounter a series of last-minute challenges that test their resolve and skills.

During a late-night working session, Elena expresses her concern about a technical bottleneck they've encountered. "This issue could affect our user experience significantly. We can't afford any missteps at launch."

Alex, though tired, remains optimistic. "Let's troubleshoot this step by step. We've overcome bigger challenges before. We can handle this." Tom, rubbing his eyes, adds, "I'll double-check the integration points again. Maybe we missed something."

Their dedication pays off as they manage to resolve the issue just in time. This victory strengthens their confidence and camaraderie, reaffirming their ability to work under pressure.

A few days before the launch, they hold a meeting to finalize their strategy. Tom brings up an important aspect. "We need to have a solid plan for handling customer feedback post-launch. It's going to be crucial for our continuous improvement."

Alex agrees, "Absolutely. Let's set up a dedicated team to monitor and address feedback. Our responsiveness will be key."

Elena suggests, "And let's use this opportunity to gather data to further refine our services. Every bit of feedback is valuable."

As the launch day arrives, the office is buzzing with excitement and a bit of nervous energy. The team gathers for a final pep talk from Alex.

"Today marks a new chapter for us," Alex begins, looking around at his team. "What we're launching is more than a platform; it's a testament to our hard work, innovation, and vision. Let's be proud of what we've achieved."

The launch event is a success, with a positive reception from users and stakeholders. The media coverage is extensive, further raising the profile of their startup in the blockchain industry.

In the aftermath of the launch, the team monitors the operation closely. They handle minor issues efficiently, demonstrating their preparedness and commitment to excellence.

A week after the launch, Alex, Elena, and Tom meet to discuss the next steps. Alex proposes,

"Now that we're up and running, it's time to think about future projects. We should continue to push the boundaries of what we can achieve with blockchain."

Elena, looking at the data from the launch, notes, "Our user base is growing rapidly. We need to ensure our infrastructure can scale with this growth."

Tom adds, "And let's not forget about exploring new applications of blockchain. There are so many possibilities."

The day begins to transition toward its conclusion, with the team poised to explore new horizons and challenges. They reflect on their journey, acknowledging the hurdles they've overcome and the lessons learned.

The final scene shows the trio in their office late at night, planning their next big project. The mood is one of determination and excitement for the future.

Alex concludes, "We've scaled new heights, but there's still so much more to achieve. Let's continue to innovate and lead the way in blockchain technology."

In the weeks following the launch, the startup experiences a significant influx of new users, bringing both excitement and new challenges. The team holds a meeting to strategize on managing this growth effectively.

During the meeting, Elena raises a concern. "Our user base has grown faster than we anticipated. We need to scale our customer support to meet this demand."

Alex nods in agreement. "You're right. Let's hire more support staff and invest in training them. We can't compromise on user experience."
Tom adds, "And with more users, we should also enhance our security protocols. The larger our platform grows, the more attractive it becomes to potential threats."

The discussion leads to a plan to strengthen their infrastructure and expand the team, ensuring the sustainability of their growth.

Meanwhile, Alex receives an invitation to speak at a prestigious technology conference, recognizing him as an influential figure in the blockchain industry. He sees this as an opportunity to not only showcase their success but also to explore potential partnerships.

During a preparation session for the conference, Tom suggests, "This is a great platform to talk about our next project. We should give them a glimpse of what we're planning next."

Alex, working on his speech, replies, "Definitely. Let's use this opportunity to spark interest in our upcoming initiatives. We're not just maintaining our current success; we're building on it."

The day of the conference arrives, and Alex takes the stage, greeted by an audience of tech enthusiasts, investors, and media. His speech highlights the success of their startup and teases exciting future projects.

After the speech, Alex is approached by several attendees interested in collaborations, offering new avenues for the startup to explore.

Back at the office, the team celebrates the successful conference. Jeff congratulates Alex, "That was an excellent presentation. You've not only raised our profile but also opened doors for new opportunities."

As the chapter progresses, the narrative explores the team's handling of these new opportunities. They conduct meetings with potential partners, carefully considering how these collaborations align with their vision and values.

Elena, in one of the meetings, points out, "While these partnerships are promising, we need to ensure they align with our commitment to social responsibility and innovation."

The day begins to transition towards its conclusion, with the team laying the groundwork for their next big project, which promises to be even more ambitious than their previous endeavors.

Alex, Elena, and Tom gather for a brainstorming session, their minds buzzing with ideas and possibilities.

Alex shares his vision, "Our journey has been incredible so far, but I feel like we're just getting started. The next chapter is about taking what we've learned and using it to make an even bigger impact."

In the wake of their recent successes and the recognition at the technology conference, Alex, Elena, and Tom find themselves at a crossroads, contemplating the next big step for their startup.

During a reflective session in their office, Alex starts, "We've achieved a lot, but the blockchain world is evolving rapidly. We need to think ahead.

What's the next big challenge we want to tackle?" Elena, always thoughtful, suggests, "I think we should delve deeper into blockchain applications in different industries.

There's potential for innovation beyond what we've already explored."

Tom, looking at recent market trends, adds, "And let's not ignore the growing interest in decentralized finance. DeFi is becoming a game-changer in the financial world. We could be at the forefront of that."

Their discussion leads to the decision to embark on a research and development phase, exploring new applications of blockchain technology in various sectors.

As they prepare for this new venture, a challenge arises in the form of a significant regulatory change that could affect the way they operate. This development necessitates a shift in their approach and strategy.

Alex, addressing the team, says, "This regulatory shift is a hurdle, but it's also an opportunity for us to innovate and adapt. Let's use this as a catalyst to explore new directions."

The narrative follows the team as they navigate these regulatory changes, consulting with legal experts and adjusting their business model to remain compliant while still pushing the boundaries of innovation.

In a meeting with Jeff, the conversation shifts towards long-term planning. Jeff advises, "You've built a strong foundation, but the key to lasting success is adaptability. Stay flexible and open to change."

As the evening draws to a close, the team begins to lay the groundwork for their new R&D initiative. They start recruiting new talent, including experts in various industries, to bring fresh perspectives to their projects.

Alex, Elena, and Tom in their office late at night, surrounded by whiteboards filled with ideas and plans. They are deep in discussion, their energy and passion for their work palpable.

Alex looks at his team and says, "We're on the brink of something big. Chapter Eight is about exploration and pushing new frontiers. Let's make it a chapter of groundbreaking innovation."

The team poised to embark on a new phase of exploration and innovation, facing regulatory challenges but undeterred in their commitment to advancing the blockchain industry. The narrative sets the stage for further developments and adventures in Chapter Eight, highlighting the team's readiness to embrace new challenges and opportunities.

Beginning Chapter Eight of "Byte Rich: The Bitcoin Odyssey," we delve into a significant event in the Bitcoin network: a contentious update leading to a division within the community. This chapter explores the concept of hard forks, governance in decentralized systems, and the resilience of open-source communities.

Chapter Eight: The Fork in the Road

Setting:
The startup's office, online forums, and community meetings related to the Bitcoin network.

Characters:
Alex: Navigates the complexities of the new situation in the Bitcoin community.

Elena and Tom: Provide technical and ethical perspectives on the issue.

Jeff: Offers guidance based on his experience.

New Characters: Members of the Bitcoin community with varying viewpoints on the network update.

Narrative:
Alex, Elena, and Tom are in the midst of a heated discussion about the recent controversial update proposed in the Bitcoin network.

Alex, looking concerned, says, "This proposed update is causing a rift in the community. Some see it as necessary for scalability, while others view it as compromising Bitcoin's core principles."

Elena adds, "It's a classic example of the challenges in decentralized governance. Without a central authority, these decisions become highly contentious."

Tom, who's been following the online discussions closely, mentions, "There's talk about a hard fork if this goes through. It could split the community and even create a new cryptocurrency."

The trio decides to host an online forum to engage with the broader Bitcoin community, aiming to understand different perspectives and foster a constructive dialogue.

During the forum, various community members express their opinions. One member, Martin, argues, "We need this update to stay relevant and competitive. Bitcoin can't stagnate."

Another member, Lisa, counters, "But at what cost? Changing the very fabric of Bitcoin's blockchain could lead us down a slippery slope."

Alex moderates the discussion, ensuring that each viewpoint is heard and respected. The debate is intense but fruitful, highlighting the diverse thought processes within the community.

Post-forum, Jeff meets with the team to discuss their stance. "In situations like these, it's crucial to consider the long-term implications. Whatever the outcome, it will set a precedent for the future of Bitcoin."

The possibility of a hard fork becomes more imminent. Alex and his team grapple with what this means for their startup and their projects, which are closely tied to the Bitcoin network.

In a strategic meeting, Elena suggests, "We should prepare for both scenarios. If a hard fork happens, we need to be ready to adapt our operations accordingly."

Tom, focusing on the community aspect, adds, "And let's use our platforms to educate our users about what this means. There's a lot of confusion and misinformation out there."

The narrative follows the unfolding events as the Bitcoin community approaches the day of the decision. Tensions are high, and the potential for a hard fork looms large.

On the decision day, the community is divided, and a hard fork occurs, creating a new cryptocurrency. The event sends ripples through the cryptocurrency world, with varying reactions from different stakeholders.

Alex, addressing his team after the fork, says, "This is a significant moment in Bitcoin's history. It's a reminder of the power and complexity of decentralized systems. We need to stay agile and responsive to these changes."

As the day nears its end, the team reflects on the resilience of the Bitcoin community and the importance of adaptability in the face of change. They begin to strategize on how to integrate this new development into their operations and services.

The late night sets the stage for the next day with Alex, Elena, and Tom planning their approach in this new landscape created by the hard fork.

Alex concludes, "A fork in the road often leads to uncharted territory. Let's navigate this new path with caution and optimism. Chapter Nine will be about adapting to change and seizing new opportunities."

In the days following the hard fork, the Bitcoin community remains in a state of flux. Alex, Elena, and Tom hold a series of meetings to discuss the implications for their startup and how to move forward in this altered environment.

During one of the meetings, Alex says, "This fork has fundamentally changed aspects of the Bitcoin network. We need to assess how this impacts our current projects and user base."

Elena, looking through data and community feedback, adds, "There's a significant split in the community. Some of our users are concerned about the stability and future of Bitcoin."

Tom suggests, "Let's host a webinar to address these concerns. We can explain what the fork means and how we plan to navigate this new phase."

The team quickly puts together a webinar, inviting their users and other interested parties.

Alex leads the session, providing clear explanations about the nature of hard forks, the reasons behind this particular split, and how it affects the broader cryptocurrency ecosystem.

After the webinar, many users express their appreciation for the clarity and support. The team feels reassured that they are maintaining trust with their user base.

In the following weeks, the startup faces the technical challenges of adapting to the new cryptocurrency created by the fork. Elena leads a task force to update their systems and ensure compatibility with both versions of Bitcoin.

During a task force meeting, Elena says, "We've managed to update our systems for compatibility with the new fork. But we need to keep a close eye on developments. The cryptocurrency landscape has become even more dynamic."

Alex acknowledges, "Great work, Elena. Let's continue to stay agile. This is a time for us to be proactive, not just reactive."

As the day progresses, the narrative explores the broader impact of the fork within the cryptocurrency market. Alex and his team observe shifts in investment, user behavior, and market dynamics.

Tom, analyzing market trends, notes, "The fork has created new investment patterns. Some see it as an opportunity, while others are more cautious. We need to understand these shifts to guide our users and our business strategy."

The team also engages with other leaders in the cryptocurrency space, participating in discussions and forums to understand the evolving landscape and contribute their perspectives.

In one such forum, Alex speaks about the importance of community in the face of change. "Events like this hard fork test the resilience of our community. It's crucial that we come together to navigate these challenges and shape the future of cryptocurrency."

As the day draws to a close, the team is seen planning their next steps, considering new project ideas that align with the changed environment.

The final scene shows the trio in a contemplative mood, reflecting on the lessons learned and the paths ahead.

Alex concludes, "The fork in the road has set us on a new path. Our next mission will be about exploring new opportunities and strengthening our position in this ever-evolving world of cryptocurrency."

As the startup navigates the post-fork cryptocurrency environment, Alex, Elena, and Tom focus on re-evaluating their long-term strategies to align with the new realities of the Bitcoin network.

In a strategy meeting, Tom brings up a key concern. "The fork has caused some instability in the market. We need to reassure our investors and stakeholders about our direction and stability."

Alex, pondering this, replies, "Agreed. Let's organize a meeting with our key investors. We'll present our updated strategy and how we plan to leverage the new opportunities arising from the fork."

Elena, reviewing their current projects, suggests, "We should also consider how these changes affect our ongoing initiatives. There might be new avenues we can explore, especially with the emergence of the new cryptocurrency."

The team organizes a meeting with their investors, where Alex leads a presentation on their adjusted business strategy. He highlights their adaptability and the potential for innovative projects in the evolving landscape.

One of the investors, Mr. Chen, expresses his support. "Your ability to swiftly adapt and rethink strategies in light of these changes is impressive. We're confident in your continued success."

Buoyed by the support of their investors, the team decides to explore new project ideas that could capitalize on the capabilities of both versions of Bitcoin.

During a brainstorming session, Elena proposes, "With the network now split, there are different technical capabilities we can explore. For instance, the new cryptocurrency has slightly different transaction properties we could utilize."

Tom adds, "And let's not ignore the community aspect. There's a whole new user base emerging around the new cryptocurrency. We could develop solutions tailored to their needs."

The narrative follows the team as they develop a new project, leveraging the unique features of the forked Bitcoin network. This project aims to enhance transaction efficiency and security, catering to a niche market that has arisen post-fork.

As they work on this new project, the team faces the challenge of balancing their resources between their existing commitments and this new initiative. Alex leads the effort to ensure a smooth transition, emphasizing the importance of efficient resource management.

In a reflective moment, Alex discusses with the team, "This new project is a leap into somewhat uncharted territory for us. But it's also a chance to demonstrate our innovative spirit and expertise."

The day begins to transition toward its end, with the team making significant progress on their new project. They conduct rigorous testing and start to create buzz in the cryptocurrency community about their upcoming solution.

The final scene of Chapter Eight shows the trio at a tech meetup, discussing their new project with intrigued attendees. The atmosphere is one of excitement and curiosity.

Alex concludes, "The path after the fork has been challenging, but it's led us to new possibilities. In Soon, we'll see the fruition of our efforts and the impact of our new project."

In the latter part of next day, the team at the startup is in high gear, preparing for the launch of their new project which capitalizes on the unique aspects of the forked Bitcoin network.

In a team meeting, Alex brings up a crucial aspect. "As we prepare for this launch, let's not forget about the importance of community engagement. The success of this project hinges not just on its technical merits but also on how well it's received by the community."

Elena, looking over the marketing plan, suggests, "We should hold a series of webinars and Q&A sessions leading up to the launch. It'll be a good way to introduce the project and address any questions or concerns."

Tom, working on the final touches of the project, adds, "And let's ensure our documentation is clear and accessible. We want users of all levels to understand and adopt our solution."

As they implement these strategies, Alex faces a new challenge. A prominent figure in the cryptocurrency community publicly expresses skepticism about their new project, questioning its viability and potential impact.

Alex decides to address this directly and arranges a live online debate with the critic. During the debate, Alex calmly and clearly explains the project's objectives, its technical foundation, and how it addresses specific needs within the cryptocurrency community.

The debate is well-received, with many viewers appreciating Alex's transparent and straightforward approach. This event helps to bolster confidence in their upcoming project.

As the launch day approaches, the team encounters a technical hiccup that threatens to delay their timeline. Working around the clock, Elena leads the effort to resolve the issue, showcasing her technical expertise and leadership skills.

Tom, exhausted but determined, says during a late-night working session, "This is one of the toughest challenges we've faced, but I know we can pull through. We've got a great team and a solid solution."

Finally, they overcome the hurdle, and the project is ready for launch. The launch event is a mix of excitement and anticipation. The cryptocurrency community, industry experts, and media are in attendance, eager to see what the team has developed.

Alex presents the new project, highlighting its innovative approach and how it addresses a niche yet significant need in the post-fork cryptocurrency landscape. The presentation is met with enthusiastic response, and the initial feedback is overwhelmingly positive.

In the aftermath of the successful launch, the team gathers to celebrate their hard work and achievement. They reflect on the journey they've taken, the challenges they've overcome, and the growth they've experienced.

Elena, raising her glass in a toast, says, "To a team that's more like a family, to challenges that make us stronger, and to a future that's brighter than ever."

The evening concludes with Alex, Elena, and Tom looking ahead, ready to tackle whatever comes next in their ever-evolving journey in the world of blockchain and cryptocurrency.

Alex closes, "We've come a long way, and there's still so much more to explore and achieve. Chapter Nine will be about taking our success to new heights and continuing to innovate."

Following the successful launch of their new project, Alex, Elena, and Tom find themselves at a juncture, reflecting on their achievements and contemplating the future direction of their startup.

In a moment of quiet after the launch celebrations, Alex shares his thoughts with the team. "This launch has been a milestone for us, but it's also a stepping stone to bigger things. We need to start thinking about what Chapter Nine holds for us."

Elena, looking thoughtful, suggests, "We've made great strides in the technical aspects of blockchain. Perhaps it's time to explore its other applications, maybe in sectors we haven't touched yet."

Tom, always keen on addressing user needs, adds, "And let's not forget about our community. They've been instrumental in our journey. Maybe we can involve them more in our future projects, get their input and ideas."

Their discussion leads to a decision to conduct a series of community workshops and brainstorming sessions, inviting users and other stakeholders to contribute ideas for future projects.

As they prepare for these sessions, the narrative follows the team grappling with the ongoing challenges of managing a rapidly growing startup.

They face decisions about scaling their team, diversifying their project portfolio, and maintaining the quality of their services.

During one of the planning meetings, Alex says, "We've always been about innovation and pushing boundaries. Let's ensure that as we grow, we don't lose that spirit."

The community workshops turn out to be a resounding success, providing the team with valuable insights and fresh perspectives. The participants, ranging from long-time blockchain enthusiasts to newcomers to the field, bring diverse ideas to the table.

One of the workshop participants, a teacher, proposes an idea. "What about using blockchain in education? There could be applications in verifying credentials or even enhancing the learning experience."

This suggestion sparks a new train of thought for the team. They begin to explore how blockchain can be leveraged in the education sector, aligning with their commitment to social impact.

As the day draws to a close, Alex, Elena, and Tom are seen brainstorming this new educational project. The atmosphere is one of excitement and possibility, as they consider the impact they could have in another important sector.

Alex addresses his team with a sense of anticipation. "The end of one chapter is the beginning of another. Chapter Nine is about exploring new horizons, about taking what we've learned and applying it in ways we've never done before. Let's embark on this new journey with the same passion and commitment that has brought us this far."

Jeff concludes with the team poised to venture into new areas of blockchain application, particularly in education, setting the stage for further innovation and exploration in Chapter Nine. The narrative emphasizes their ongoing commitment to growth, learning, and community engagement.

Beginning Chapter Nine of "Byte Rich: The Bitcoin Odyssey," titled "Rigging the Game," we revisit an earlier phase in the trio's journey, focusing on a pivotal moment when they assembled their first mining rig. This chapter provides an insightful look into the technology and process behind Bitcoin mining.

Chapter Nine: Rigging the Game

Setting:
Flashback to the early days of the trio's venture into Bitcoin mining, in Alex's garage turned makeshift workshop.

Characters:
Alex: Eager and determined to build his first mining rig.

Elena and Tom: Assisting Alex in the assembly process, contributing their respective expertise.

New Characters: Hardware suppliers and tech experts whom the trio consults.

Narrative:
As the day opens, Alex, Elena, and Tom are seen in Alex's garage, surrounded by computer parts, tools, and manuals. The atmosphere is filled with a sense of determination and anticipation.

Alex, examining a motherboard, says, "This is where it all begins. Building our mining rig from scratch is going to be a challenge, but it's the only way we can really understand the nuts and bolts of Bitcoin mining."

Elena, organizing the GPUs (Graphics Processing Units), adds, "These GPUs are the heart of our mining rig. They'll handle the complex calculations required for mining Bitcoin."

Tom, looking over the power supply units, remarks, "And we need to ensure we have enough power and cooling. Mining rigs consume a lot of electricity and generate a lot of heat."

The narrative delves into the detailed process of assembling the mining rig. Alex and his team encounter various challenges, from compatibility issues between components to optimizing the configuration for maximum efficiency.

During the assembly, they consult with various hardware suppliers and tech experts, gaining deeper insights into the workings of mining hardware and the technology behind Bitcoin.

As they progress, Elena brings up a concern. "We need to consider the cost of running this rig, not just in terms of power consumption but also the potential wear and tear on the equipment."

Alex nods, "You're right. Let's track our expenses and calculate the potential return on investment. We need to know if this is sustainable in the long run."

After several days of work, the trio finally completes the assembly of their first mining rig. The moment they power it up is filled with excitement and a bit of anxiety.

Tom, watching the screens as the rig boots up, exclaims, "It's working! The rig is operational, and we're officially mining Bitcoin!"

The day continues with the trio monitoring their first mining rig, making adjustments and optimizations as they learn more about the intricacies of Bitcoin mining.

One evening, as they review the performance data, Alex reflects, "Building this rig has been more than just a technical challenge. It's taught us about patience, persistence, and the intricacies of the Bitcoin network."

As the evening draws to a close, the narrative begins to transition to the next chapter. The experience of building and operating their first mining rig lays the foundation for the trio's deeper venture into the world of cryptocurrency.

Alex, Elena, and Tom are gathered around their rig, discussing plans to expand their mining operation. Alex concludes the chapter, "This rig is just the start. As we scale up our operation and face new challenges as we dive deeper into the world of cryptocurrency mining."

After successfully assembling their first mining rig, Alex, Elena, and Tom begin to plan the expansion of their mining operation. The garage, once a small workshop, is slowly transforming into a more sophisticated mining hub.

In a planning session, Tom looks at the power bills and expresses a concern, "Our electricity costs are rising with the new rig. We need to find a way to make our operation more energy-efficient."

Elena, researching alternative solutions, suggests, "What about exploring renewable energy sources? Solar power could reduce our costs and make our mining operation more sustainable."

Alex nods in agreement. "It's a good idea. Let's look into solar panels and other green solutions. It aligns with our commitment to sustainability."

The narrative then follows the team as they investigate and invest in solar energy, setting up panels to power their mining rigs. This transition poses its own set of challenges, from the technical setup to understanding the dynamics of solar energy.

During the installation, Alex has a conversation with the solar panel supplier, Mr. Singh. "We're excited about this transition to solar power. It's new territory for us."

Mr. Singh replies, "You're making a wise choice. Solar energy is not only cost-effective in the long run, but it also reduces your carbon footprint. More businesses should follow your example."

As their mining operation becomes more energy-efficient and environmentally friendly, the trio starts to attract attention from the local community and the broader Bitcoin network.

They receive inquiries and visits from other miners and enthusiasts interested in their setup.

In one such visit, a fellow miner, Lydia, asks, "I've heard about your solar-powered mining rig. How effective has it been in terms of cost and mining efficiency?"

Elena responds, "It's been a learning curve, but we've managed to reduce our electricity costs significantly. Plus, it feels good to know we're mining in a more environmentally responsible way."

As the day progresses, the team faces the reality of the highly competitive nature of Bitcoin mining. The difficulty of mining increases, and the rewards become harder to earn.

Alex, reflecting on this challenge, says, "Bitcoin mining is becoming increasingly competitive. We need to constantly innovate and adapt our strategies if we want to stay in the game."

Elena adds, "And let's not forget the importance of staying up-to-date with the latest technology. We should consider upgrading our rigs to stay efficient."

The day begins to transition towards its conclusion with the team planning further expansions and upgrades to their mining operation. They discuss new technologies, potential partnerships, and strategies to maintain their competitiveness in the mining landscape.

Alex, Elena, and Tom are seen discussing their future plans, their faces lit by the glow of their mining rigs.

Alex concludes, "Our journey in mining has been full of challenges, but also full of rewards. In Chapter Ten, we'll explore new frontiers in mining and continue to innovate in this ever-evolving landscape."

As their mining operation grows, Alex, Elena, and Tom start exploring advanced mining technologies, including the latest ASIC (Application-Specific Integrated Circuit) miners, which offer higher efficiency and processing power.

In a discussion about this upgrade, Elena expresses her thoughts. "Switching to ASIC miners is a significant investment, but it's necessary. The increased hash rate could really boost our mining rewards."

Tom, always cautious about financial decisions, adds, "We need to balance our investment with the potential returns. The crypto market is volatile, and we should avoid overextending ourselves."

Alex, looking at the broader picture, suggests, "Let's run a cost-benefit analysis. We need to ensure that this move aligns with our long-term strategy and doesn't just cater to short-term gains."

The trio decides to proceed with the purchase of ASIC miners after thorough research and financial planning. As they integrate these new machines into their operation, they face the challenge of configuring and optimizing them for peak performance.

During one of their setup sessions, Tom encounters a technical issue with the configuration. "These ASIC miners are more complex than I anticipated. We might need to consult with an expert to optimize their performance."

Alex agrees, "Let's do that. It's important to maximize their efficiency from the start."

They reach out to a renowned crypto mining expert, Dr. Amelia Rios, for guidance. In a consultation session, Dr. Rios shares valuable insights into optimizing ASIC miners and the latest trends in crypto mining.

Dr. Rios advises, "Keep an eye on the market and mining difficulty. Your strategies should be adaptable to these changes. Also, consider joining a larger mining pool to increase your chances of earning rewards."

Armed with this new knowledge, the team successfully optimizes their ASIC miners and joins a more prominent mining pool, further enhancing their operation's effectiveness.

As the day progresses, the trio's expanded mining operation begins to yield higher rewards.

However, they remain mindful of the environmental impact and continue to invest in sustainable practices.

One evening, while reviewing their operation's performance, Elena raises a concern. "Our success is great, but we should also think about giving back to the community. Maybe we can fund blockchain education initiatives or support tech startups."

Tom agrees, "That's a great idea. Our growth shouldn't just be about profit. We have the resources to make a positive impact."

The narrative begins to transition towards the end of the chapter, with the team planning how to reinvest part of their profits into community projects and sustainable initiatives.

Alex, Elena, and Tom are seen in a local community center, where they sponsor a workshop on blockchain technology for young students.

Alex concludes, "Our journey in Bitcoin mining has taught us a lot. But the real reward is using what we've learned and earned to empower others. In Chapter Ten, we'll continue to expand our horizons and use our success to foster growth and innovation in the blockchain community."

In the latter part of the week, Alex, Elena, and Tom focus on balancing their expanding mining operations with their dedication to ethical and sustainable practices.

During a team meeting, Alex reflects on their progress. "Our mining operation is more successful than ever, but it's crucial we stay true to our values. Let's brainstorm ways to keep our impact positive."

Elena, who has been researching sustainable energy solutions, suggests, "We could explore additional renewable energy sources. Perhaps wind or hydro power could complement our solar setup."

Tom, thinking about community engagement, adds, "And what about organizing more educational workshops? We can share our knowledge about blockchain and its potential beyond just cryptocurrency."

The team decides to allocate a portion of their profits to expanding their renewable energy setup and organizing community outreach programs.

They work on a detailed plan to implement these initiatives over the coming months.

As they proceed with these plans, a new challenge arises in the form of a sudden market downturn, which affects the profitability of their mining operation. The team convenes to discuss how to navigate this new challenge.

Alex starts the discussion, "This downturn is a reminder of the volatility in the crypto market. We need to adjust our strategy to ensure our operation remains sustainable."

Elena, analyzing the market trends, notes, "We might need to scale back some of our operations temporarily. It's about long-term sustainability, not just short-term gains."

Tom, concerned about the community projects, asks, "Can we continue our outreach programs and renewable energy investments in this market condition?"

Alex responds, "These initiatives are important to us. We'll find a way to keep them going. It's about balancing our priorities."

The narrative follows the team as they make strategic adjustments to their mining operation, reducing costs where possible while maintaining their commitment to their community and sustainability projects.

In a community workshop, Alex shares insights about the volatile nature of cryptocurrencies and the importance of resilience and adaptability in this field. The attendees, ranging from enthusiastic amateurs to seasoned professionals, appreciate the honest and practical advice.

Towards the end of the chapter, the market begins to stabilize, and the trio's adjustments pay off. Their mining operation regains profitability, and their community initiatives receive positive feedback.

The team gathers to review their progress. They discuss future plans, including the possibility of exploring new blockchain technologies and expanding their educational outreach.

Alex concludes, "Every challenge we face teaches us something valuable. In Chapter Ten, we'll take these lessons and continue to grow, not just as a business but as a force for positive change in the blockchain community."

Alex, Elena, and Tom are reflecting on their journey so far and preparing for the next big phase of their venture. They recognize the need to adapt to the ever-changing landscape of cryptocurrency and blockchain technology.

In a strategy meeting, Alex proposes a new direction. "We've made great strides in mining and community outreach. Now, I think it's time to explore new applications of blockchain. We should consider branching out into areas like smart contracts or decentralized applications." Elena, enthusiastic about the idea, adds, "Expanding into new blockchain applications could really diversify our portfolio. It's a natural progression for us."

Tom, always thoughtful about practical implications, says, "Let's conduct thorough market research. We need to understand where we can have the most impact and what resources we'll need."

The team agrees to allocate time and resources to research and development in these new areas.

They also decide to hire additional talent to support this expansion, bringing fresh perspectives and expertise to their team.

As they prepare for this new venture, the trio holds a community event to share their plans and gather feedback. The event is well-attended, with many expressing excitement about the startup's new direction.

During the event, a community member asks Alex, "How do you ensure that you stay ahead in such a fast-paced industry?"

Alex responds, "It's about continuous learning and adapting. We stay open to new ideas and constantly challenge our own assumptions. That's how we keep evolving."

The narrative then shifts to the team setting the groundwork for their new projects. They delve into research on various blockchain technologies, potential partnerships, and market needs.

In one of their research sessions, Elena brings up an interesting point. "Blockchain technology has so much potential in areas like digital identity and supply chain management. These could be promising avenues for us."

Tom, looking at the latest blockchain trends, suggests, "And let's not ignore the growing interest in decentralized finance. There could be opportunities there for us too."

As the day draws to a close, the team starts laying the foundation for their next chapter. They are seen brainstorming, planning, and preparing for the challenges and opportunities that lie ahead in the realm of blockchain technology.

Alex, Elena, and Tom are in their office late at night, surrounded by whiteboards filled with ideas and plans.

Alex concludes, "Our journey so far has been incredible, but I have a feeling that the best is yet to come. In Chapter Ten, we'll dive into these new blockchain territories, pushing the boundaries of what's possible."

The day concludes with the trio poised on the brink of exploring new applications in blockchain technology, emphasizing their commitment to innovation and growth. The narrative sets the stage for further exploration and impact in the world of blockchain in Chapter Ten.

Beginning Chapter Ten of "Byte Rich: The Bitcoin Odyssey," titled "The Value of a Byte," we delve into the trio's experiences with the fluctuating value of Bitcoin. This chapter explores economic concepts like market volatility, supply and demand, and the impact of external events on cryptocurrency.

Chapter Ten: The Value of a Byte

Setting:
The startup's office, various financial and cryptocurrency forums, and meetings with economic experts.

Characters:
Alex: Analyzes and responds to the volatile Bitcoin market.

Elena and Tom: Offer their perspectives on the economic factors affecting cryptocurrency.

Jeff: Provides mentorship and insights into market dynamics.

New Characters: Financial analysts, economists, and other cryptocurrency experts.

Narrative:
The day opens with Alex, Elena, and Tom in a meeting, discussing a sudden drop in Bitcoin's value. The mood is tense as they analyze the market charts.

Alex, trying to maintain a level head, says, "This drop is significant. We need to understand what's driving this volatility. Is it a market correction, or are there external factors at play?"

Elena, who has been researching recent market trends, adds, "It looks like a combination of factors. There's been some negative press around cryptocurrencies, and a few major economies are considering regulatory changes."

Tom, looking at their operation's financials, points out, "We need to be prepared for these fluctuations. Our revenue is closely tied to Bitcoin's value, and these ups and downs affect our bottom line."

The trio decides to consult with financial analysts and economists to gain a deeper understanding of the situation. In a meeting with one such analyst, Mr. Dawson, they discuss the complexities of the cryptocurrency market.

Mr. Dawson explains, "Cryptocurrencies like Bitcoin are still relatively new. They're subject to market dynamics like supply and demand, but they're also highly influenced by public perception and regulatory environments."

Alex asks, "How can we mitigate the risks associated with such volatility?"

Mr. Dawson advises, "Diversification is key. Don't put all your eggs in one basket. Also, stay informed and agile. The cryptocurrency market is unpredictable, and quick responses are crucial."

Following this advice, the team starts exploring ways to diversify their investment and revenue streams. They also increase their focus on staying abreast of global economic trends and regulatory changes.

In a subsequent team meeting, Elena suggests, "We should consider expanding into other cryptocurrencies or blockchain applications. It's a way to hedge against Bitcoin's volatility."

Tom, thinking about the bigger picture, adds, "And let's not forget about our user base. We should educate them about market volatility and responsible investment in cryptocurrencies."

The narrative then follows the team as they implement these strategies, including launching educational webinars for their users and investing in research for new blockchain projects.

Bitcoin's value begins to stabilize, and the team's efforts to adapt to the market volatility pay off. Their diversified approach helps them weather the storm and positions them for future growth.

In a reflective moment, Alex discusses with the team, "The cryptocurrency market is a rollercoaster, but it's also full of opportunities. Staying informed, adaptable, and diversified is how we'll continue to thrive."

As the evening nears its end, the narrative begins to transition towards the next stage. The team is seen planning for the future, armed with the knowledge and experience gained from navigating the volatile cryptocurrency market.

Alex, Elena, and Tom are in their office, looking at the latest market data and discussing potential new blockchain projects.

Alex concludes the chapter, "Our journey through the highs and lows of Bitcoin's value has taught us invaluable lessons. In Chapter Eleven, we'll use these insights to explore new frontiers in blockchain and cryptocurrency."

As the day progresses, Alex, Elena, and Tom focus on developing a more robust strategy to insulate their startup from the extreme fluctuations of the cryptocurrency market.

In a strategy session, Tom brings up an important point. "We've seen how external events can impact Bitcoin's value. We should start monitoring global economic trends more closely, as they can give us early warning signs."

Elena, working on a new data analytics model, suggests, "I've been developing this tool to analyze market trends and predict potential shifts. It might help us in making more informed decisions."

Alex, impressed with Elena's initiative, says, "That's excellent, Elena. Let's integrate it into our decision-making process. Being proactive is better than reacting to market changes after the fact."

The team starts to use Elena's tool, which helps them anticipate and respond to market dynamics more effectively. This proactive approach allows them to make strategic adjustments to their operations, minimizing the impact of market volatility.

During this period, Alex decides to diversify their investment portfolio. He explores opportunities in other cryptocurrencies and blockchain-related ventures that show potential for stable growth.

In a discussion about diversification, Alex says, "Diversifying our portfolio will help us mitigate the risks associated with Bitcoin's volatility. We should look at cryptocurrencies with different use cases and market dynamics."

Elena adds, "And let's not limit ourselves to just cryptocurrencies. Blockchain technology has applications in various fields. We can invest in startups that are using blockchain in innovative ways."

The team attends a blockchain technology summit, where they network with other professionals and entrepreneurs in the field. This summit provides them with insights into emerging trends and potential investment opportunities.

At the summit, Tom engages in a conversation with a representative from a blockchain-based supply chain management startup. "Your approach to using blockchain for supply chain transparency is fascinating. There might be synergy between our projects."

The narrative then shifts to the team making strategic investments in a few selected startups and cryptocurrencies, broadening their business scope and reducing dependency on Bitcoin's market performance.

As they implement these changes, they continue their educational initiatives, sharing their learning and experiences with their user base. They host webinars and write articles on understanding market volatility and the importance of a diversified investment strategy in the world of cryptocurrency.

The team reflects on their growth and the lessons learned from navigating the highs and lows of Bitcoin's value.

Alex, in a moment of introspection, shares with Elena and Tom, "This journey has taught us about resilience, adaptability, and the importance of foresight. As we step into Chapter Eleven, we're better equipped to face whatever challenges and opportunities come our way."

The startup faces the challenge of managing its growing portfolio of investments and projects. Alex, Elena, and Tom hold frequent strategy meetings to ensure they stay aligned with their vision while adapting to the market's volatility.

In one such meeting, Alex expresses his vision for the future. "Our growth has been phenomenal, but with growth comes complexity. We need to ensure we're not spreading ourselves too thin."

Elena, looking over their project timelines, adds, "Prioritization is key. We should focus our energy on projects with the most potential impact and align them with our core values."

Tom, who has been monitoring the latest developments in blockchain technology, suggests, "We should also keep an eye on emerging technologies like non-fungible tokens (NFTs) and decentralized finance (DeFi). These areas are gaining momentum rapidly."

The narrative then explores how the trio allocates resources to different projects, making tough decisions to phase out less promising ventures and double down on those with more potential.

Amid these strategic shifts, the team encounters a new challenge: a cybersecurity threat to their mining operation. They mobilize quickly to address the issue, reinforcing the importance of robust security measures in their business.

In a debriefing session after resolving the threat, Tom emphasizes the lesson learned. "This incident was a wake-up call. As we expand, our exposure to risks increases. We need to invest more in our cybersecurity infrastructure."

Alex, concerned about the potential impact of such threats, agrees, "Absolutely. Let's bring in a cybersecurity expert to audit our systems and recommend enhancements. We can't afford to take any chances."

As the weeks progress, the team successfully enhances their security protocols, fortifying their operations against future threats. This proactive approach reinforces their commitment to maintaining a safe and reliable platform for their users.

Alex, Elena, and Tom start to see the fruits of their diversified strategy. Their investments in other blockchain ventures begin to show promising results, and their educational initiatives are well-received by the community, establishing them as thought leaders in the blockchain space.

In a reflective conversation, Elena shares, "It's amazing to see how far we've come. We started with a simple mining operation, and now we're influencing different facets of the blockchain world."

Alex, looking at their roadmap, adds, "Our journey has been full of ups and downs, but each challenge has only made us stronger. We're not just surviving in this market; we're thriving."

The next day shows the trio at a major blockchain conference where they are invited to speak. They share their journey and insights, inspiring a new generation of blockchain enthusiasts and entrepreneurs.

Alex concludes, "Our story is a testament to the power of perseverance, innovation, and adaptability. We continue to build on this foundation, exploring new territories and breaking new ground in the blockchain ecosystem."

In the latter part of the next day, as the trio enjoys the success of their diversified blockchain ventures, an unexpected challenge looms on the horizon. During a routine check, Tom discovers unusual activity in their system, indicating a potential security breach.

Tom urgently calls Alex and Elena to the monitoring room. "Guys, we might have a problem. I've detected some unauthorized access in our network. It looks like a sophisticated hack attempt."

Alex, immediately grasping the severity of the situation, says, "Let's not jump to conclusions. First, we need to assess the extent of the breach and then contain it."

Elena, already on her laptop, adds, "I'm running a diagnostic. We'll need to trace the source of this breach. Every minute counts now."

The team works tirelessly, implementing their cybersecurity protocols. Despite their efforts, they soon realize that the attack is more serious than they initially thought. Sensitive data is at risk, and the integrity of their operations is compromised.

In a moment of tension, Alex calls an emergency meeting. "This attack is a direct threat to our users' trust in us. We need to handle this with transparency and urgency."

Elena, looking over the data, updates, "We've managed to isolate the affected systems, but we're not out of the woods yet. We need to enhance our security measures to prevent future attacks." Tom, concerned about the public reaction, suggests, "We should issue a statement to our users, explaining the situation and what we're doing to resolve it. It's important to maintain open communication."

The trio works with their cybersecurity team to resolve the hack. They also communicate with their users, keeping them informed about the situation and the measures being taken.

As they navigate through this crisis, the narrative explores the technical and ethical challenges they face. The hack attack tests their skills, their commitment to their users, and their resilience as a team.

In a late-night strategy session, Alex reflects on the experience. "This attack has been a harsh reminder of the vulnerabilities in the digital world. But it's also shown us the importance of being prepared and responsive."

Elena, looking ahead, adds, "We've learned valuable lessons from this. Our focus now should be on strengthening our defenses and rebuilding any lost trust with our users."

As the evening draws to a close, the team successfully mitigates the hack attack, but the incident leaves a lasting impact. It serves as a catalyst for them to reevaluate and enhance their security measures.

In the final scene, the trio is seen planning a comprehensive overhaul of their cybersecurity strategies, preparing for the challenges that Chapter Eleven will bring.

Alex concludes, "The hack attack was a wake-up call. In'The Hack Attack,' we'll turn this challenge into an opportunity to come back stronger and more secure than ever."

Chapter Ten concludes with the team facing a significant cybersecurity challenge, setting the stage for a deeper exploration of digital security and resilience in the upcoming chapter. The narrative highlights the importance of preparedness and adaptability in the face of cyber threats.

Beginning Chapter Eleven of "Byte Rich: The Bitcoin Odyssey," titled "Hack Attack," we delve into the aftermath of a significant hacking incident at a major Bitcoin exchange. This chapter underscores the theme of cybersecurity and the critical importance of secure digital practices for Alex and his team.

Chapter Eleven: Hack Attack

Setting:
The startup's office in the aftermath of the
hacking incident, cybersecurity meetings, and
digital security workshops.

Characters:
Alex: Deeply involved in addressing the hack and
reinforcing digital security.

Elena and Tom: Actively working on enhancing security measures and learning from the incident.

Jeff: Provides guidance and support in navigating the crisis.

New Characters: Cybersecurity experts and IT forensic analysts.

Narrative:
Alex, Elena, and Tom are in a state of high alert following the hacking incident. The team has gathered in the office, along with a team of cybersecurity experts, to assess the damage and reinforce their digital security.

Alex, looking over the preliminary reports, says gravely, "This hack was more sophisticated than we anticipated. It's not just our operations that were targeted; our users' data was also compromised."

Elena, analyzing the data, adds, "The hackers exploited a vulnerability in our software. We need to patch this immediately and review all our systems for any other potential weaknesses."

Tom, concerned about the broader implications, notes, "This isn't just about us. It shakes trust in the entire Bitcoin network. We need to be part of the solution in restoring that trust."

The narrative follows the team as they work tirelessly to secure their systems. They collaborate with cybersecurity experts to conduct a thorough investigation into the breach and implement enhanced security protocols.

In a meeting with a cybersecurity expert, Dr. Susan Choi, Alex asks, "How can we prevent such incidents in the future? What steps can we take to fortify our defenses?"

Dr. Choi advises, "It's about layers of security. You need to have multiple defenses in place – encryption, firewalls, regular audits, and most importantly, a culture of security awareness among your team."

Following this advice, the team initiates a series of workshops for their staff, focusing on cybersecurity best practices, phishing attack prevention, and secure coding techniques.

As they implement these measures, Elena leads an initiative to communicate with their users about the breach. "We need to be transparent with our users about what happened and what we're doing to protect their data."

Tom works on crafting a comprehensive communication strategy to inform their users, address their concerns, and rebuild trust.

The chapter then explores the broader impact of the hack on the Bitcoin community. The team attends a summit on cryptocurrency security, where they share their experience and learn from others who have faced similar challenges.

During a panel discussion at the summit, Alex shares, "This hack was a hard lesson, but it's also been a catalyst for change. We're now more committed than ever to ensuring the security and integrity of our operations."

The narrative then shifts to the team's ongoing efforts to enhance their cybersecurity posture. They collaborate with other businesses in the cryptocurrency space to develop industry-wide security standards.

As the evening draws to a close, the team reflects on the lessons learned from the hack. They recognize that cybersecurity is an ongoing journey, requiring constant vigilance and adaptation.

In the final scene, Alex, Elena, and Tom are seen implementing the latest cybersecurity technologies and practices, determined to safeguard their operation and contribute to the security of the wider Bitcoin network.

Alex concludes, "The hack attack tested us in ways we never expected. In Chapter Twelve, we'll continue to strengthen our defenses and be proactive in the face of new challenges."

In a detailed analysis session with Dr. Choi, the cybersecurity expert, Alex, Elena, and Tom learn about the specifics of the hack. Dr. Choi explains various common crypto hacking strategies, shedding light on how the attackers might have breached their system.

Dr. Choi begins, "One common attack vector in crypto hacks is through phishing. Hackers trick employees into revealing sensitive information or gaining access to secure environments."

Elena, recalling the incident, says, "We did find a phishing email that was opened by one of our team members. It seemed to be the entry point for the breach."

Dr. Choi nods, "That's a likely start. Hackers then probably used that access to exploit vulnerabilities in your software. Another common method is injecting malicious code or using ransomware."

Tom, concerned about future threats, asks, "How can we protect ourselves against these kinds of attacks?"

"The key is a combination of technology and training," Dr. Choi advises. "Use advanced anti-phishing tools, regularly update and patch your systems, and most importantly, train your staff to recognize and report potential security threats."

The narrative then follows the team as they implement comprehensive cybersecurity measures. They invest in advanced security software, conduct regular system audits, and initiate ongoing staff training programs.

Alex, in a team meeting, emphasizes the importance of vigilance. "Cybersecurity is not just the responsibility of our IT department. It's everyone's business. We all need to be alert and informed."

As they fortify their defenses, the team also explores the broader implications of cybersecurity in the cryptocurrency space. They engage with other industry leaders to discuss collaborative approaches to enhancing security across the network.

In a roundtable discussion with other crypto businesses, Elena shares their experience. "Our recent hack taught us a lot. We're now more committed to working with others in the industry to develop shared security protocols."

The discussion leads to the formation of an industry-wide cybersecurity coalition, with the goal of sharing knowledge, resources, and best practices to safeguard the entire cryptocurrency ecosystem.

The team's efforts start to pay off. Their enhanced security measures prove effective, and they regain the trust of their users and stakeholders.

In a reflective moment, Tom looks back on the journey. "This hack was a brutal challenge, but it made us stronger. We've not only improved our own security but also contributed to making the whole cryptocurrency network safer."

As the evening closes, the trio is seen participating in a global cybersecurity conference, where they are recognized for their proactive response to the hack and their contributions to industry-wide security efforts.

Alex concludes, "The hack attack was a turning point for us. Well continue to build on our learnings, exploring new technologies and strategies to stay ahead in this ever-evolving cybersecurity landscape."

In a detailed debriefing session, Alex, Elena, Tom, and Dr. Choi analyze the forensic reports of the hack. They discover that the intrusion was more sophisticated than initially thought, involving a series of layered attacks.

Dr. Choi explains, "The attackers used a multi-vector approach. After the initial phishing breach, they exploited a zero-day vulnerability in your system, which allowed them to bypass security measures undetected."

Alex, concerned about preventing future incidents, asks, "How can we safeguard against such complex attacks?"

Dr. Choi responds, "It's about building a multi-layered defense strategy. Apart from technical solutions, you need to foster a security-first culture within your organization."

Elena, taking notes, suggests, "We should conduct regular penetration tests and security audits. Identifying vulnerabilities before attackers do is crucial."

Tom adds, "And let's review our incident response plan. We need to be able to react quickly and effectively if something like this happens again."

The narrative then follows the team as they implement these recommendations. They partner with a cybersecurity firm to conduct regular penetration testing and upgrade their security systems with advanced threat detection and response capabilities.

In one of their training sessions for staff, Elena emphasizes the importance of vigilance. "Every email, every download, every login attempt could be a potential threat. Always be cautious and verify before you click or share information."

The team also revises their incident response protocol, ensuring a swift and coordinated reaction to any future security breaches.

As they delve deeper into the investigation, they uncover that the attack was part of a larger scheme targeting several major players in the cryptocurrency market. This revelation leads them to collaborate with other affected organizations to share insights and strengthen defenses collectively.

In a meeting with other crypto businesses, Alex shares their experience. "Collaboration is key in cybersecurity. By sharing our experiences and strategies, we can protect not just ourselves but the entire crypto ecosystem."

The day progresses with the team taking proactive measures to educate their users about cybersecurity. They launch a series of user-friendly guides and webinars on digital security practices, contributing to the wider community's knowledge and preparedness.

The efforts in enhancing cybersecurity start to show positive results. Their systems are more secure, their staff more aware, and their users better informed.

In a moment of reflection, Tom acknowledges the journey. "This hack was a brutal lesson, but it pushed us to become better. We're now at the forefront of cybersecurity in the crypto space."

As the evening concludes, the trio prepares for a cybersecurity summit where they are invited to speak about their experiences and the lessons they've learned.

Alex concludes "Our journey through this hack attack has been challenging, but it's taught us invaluable lessons. In Chapter Twelve, we'll continue to leverage these learnings, advancing not just our security but also our innovation in blockchain technology."

In the weeks following the resolution of the hacking incident, the trio dedicates time to review and internalize the lessons learned, focusing on strengthening their operation against future threats.

In a reflective meeting, Alex starts the discussion. "This hack has been a tough teacher. One key lesson for me is the importance of continuous vigilance. We can't afford to let our guard down, even for a moment."

Elena, who has been working closely with the IT team, adds, "I've learned that security isn't just about having the right tools; it's about having the right mindset. Every member of our team needs to be a part of our security strategy."

Tom, looking over the revised security protocols, says, "And the importance of having a robust incident response plan cannot be overstated. Our ability to respond quickly and effectively made a big difference."

The narrative then explores how the team implements these lessons into their daily operations. They establish regular training sessions for all staff, focusing on cybersecurity awareness and best practices. These sessions cover topics like identifying phishing attempts, securing personal and professional data, and the importance of regular password updates.

In one of these training sessions, a team member asks Alex, "How can we be sure that we're really safe from hackers?"

Alex responds, "Absolute security is a myth, but that doesn't mean we can't be well-prepared. It's about layering our defenses and being ready to adapt and respond to new threats."

The team also revisits their technological infrastructure, investing in more advanced security software and services. They work with cybersecurity experts to ensure their systems are as secure as possible, implementing measures like two-factor authentication, end-to-end encryption, and regular system audits.

Elena leads an initiative to develop a more comprehensive disaster recovery plan. "We need to be prepared for the worst-case scenario. Our recovery plan should minimize downtime and data loss in the event of another attack."

As the evening progresses, the trio also recognizes the importance of transparency and communication in building trust. They make it a priority to keep their users informed about security measures and any potential risks.

Tom, during a webinar with users, explains, "We want you to know that protecting your data is our top priority. We're committed to transparency and will keep you updated about any security developments."

By the end of the day, the team has emerged stronger and more resilient. They have not only fortified their defenses but also fostered a culture of security within their organization and among their users.

In the concluding scene, Alex, Elena, and Tom review the progress they've made since the hack. They discuss future plans and strategies, now more aware and prepared for the challenges of the digital world.

"The hack attack was a defining moment for us. We've emerged more knowledgeable and resilient. We will continue to build on these foundations, pushing forward with innovation and security hand in hand."

In the wake of the hacking incident, Alex, Elena, and Tom take proactive steps to enhance their cybersecurity measures and skills. They recognize the need for a multifaceted approach that includes technological upgrades, team skill development, and a proactive security culture.

In a dedicated meeting to discuss new security strategies, Alex says, "Our first step is to implement new prevention procedures. We need cutting-edge security tools that can identify and neutralize threats before they become a problem."

Elena, who has been researching various cybersecurity technologies, suggests, "We should invest in an intrusion detection system (IDS) and an intrusion prevention system (IPS). These will give us real-time monitoring capabilities and automatic threat mitigation."

Tom, focusing on the human element, adds, "Technology is crucial, but we also need to enhance our team's skills. I propose we bring in experts to train us in 'white hat' hacking techniques. Understanding how hackers think will help us defend against them."

The team decides to hire a cybersecurity firm to conduct intensive 'white hat' hacking workshops. These sessions involve learning about and practicing ethical hacking techniques, vulnerability assessments, and penetration testing.

As the day progresses, the narrative follows the team through their rigorous training. They learn to think like hackers, enabling them to anticipate potential security breaches and reinforce their defenses accordingly.

During one of the training sessions, a cybersecurity expert, Mr. Larson, challenges the team with a mock hacking scenario. "Think like the attacker. How would you exploit this system's vulnerabilities? Understanding this will help you fortify it."

Elena, engaged in the exercise, realizes, "It's like a chess game. Anticipating the opponent's moves is key."

The team also focuses on building a more robust IT department. They recruit new talents, including cybersecurity specialists and network engineers, to ensure they have the expertise needed to maintain and enhance their security posture.

Alex, in a team-building session, shares his vision. "With these new additions to our team and our ongoing training, we're not just recovering from the hack; we're building a team that's ready for the future."

As they implement these changes, the team starts to see the results. Their systems are more secure, their response time to potential threats improves, and the overall awareness of cybersecurity within the organization grows significantly.

In a later meeting, Tom reflects on their progress. "We've come a long way since the hack. Our new procedures and the skills we've developed have made us stronger."

As the evening nears its conclusion, the team looks forward to an exciting future. They have transformed a crisis into a catalyst for growth, emerging as a more resilient and skilled group, ready to tackle new challenges in the blockchain space.

Alex concludes, "We've turned a setback into a stepping stone. Chapter Twelve will see us apply these new skills and strategies as we continue to innovate and lead in the world of cryptocurrency."

The week concludes with the team having significantly enhanced their cybersecurity posture and skills, setting the stage for new challenges and innovations in the next chapter. The narrative emphasizes their resilience, adaptability, and commitment to continuous learning and improvement.

Chapter Twelve: Full Circle

Setting:
A mix of settings including the startup's office, a
major blockchain conference, and a quiet
reflective space where Alex looks back on the
journey.

Characters:
Alex: Reflecting on his journey and the lessons learned.

Elena and Tom: Sharing their experiences and looking forward to the future.

Jeff: Offering final words of wisdom and encouragement.

New Characters: Other members of the cryptocurrency and blockchain community, reflecting on the growth of the sector.

Narrative:
Alex is seen in a quiet room, gazing at a framed photo of him, Elena, and Tom taken during their early days of Bitcoin mining. He is reflective, thoughtful about the journey they have undertaken.

Alex muses to himself, "It's been an incredible journey. From a small mining rig in a garage to a leading startup in the blockchain space. We've faced challenges, but each one has made us stronger."

The scene shifts to a major blockchain conference where Alex, Elena, and Tom are invited as keynote speakers. They share their journey with a large audience, highlighting the ups and downs, the innovations, and the lessons learned along the way.

During the panel, Elena says, "Our journey with Bitcoin and blockchain has been about more than just technology. It's been a journey of growth, learning, and community building."

Tom adds, "We've seen the ecosystem evolve, adapt, and grow. It's been a privilege to be a part of this revolution and to contribute to its development."

Post-conference, the trio gathers in a quiet café, reminiscing about their early days and discussing the future. Alex brings up the topic of their next venture, "We've achieved a lot, but there's still so much more to explore in blockchain technology.

What's the next challenge we want to tackle?" Elena, always forward-thinking, suggests, "Let's focus on blockchain applications that can have a social impact. We have the opportunity to use this technology for good, to address real-world problems."
Tom, enthusiastic about the idea, adds, "Absolutely. Let's use our skills and resources to make a difference. That's been the most rewarding part of our journey."

As they discuss potential projects, Jeff joins them, offering his insights and encouragement.

"You've come full circle, but the journey doesn't end here. The future of blockchain is bright, and you have a pivotal role to play in shaping it."

Alex, Elena, and Tom embarking on their new project, fueled by the same passion and determination that started their journey. They are seen collaborating with other leaders in the blockchain space, committed to driving positive change through technology.

In the concluding moments, Alex reflects on their journey to an audience at a blockchain event. "Our story with Bitcoin and blockchain is a testament to the power of perseverance, innovation, and collaboration. We started with a simple dream, and it's led us here. The future is unwritten, and it's ours to shape."

In the serene ambiance of the café, post-conference, Alex, Elena, and Tom engage in a heartfelt discussion about their future direction and the impact they wish to make in the blockchain space.
Alex, with a sense of nostalgia and anticipation, shares, "Looking back, I realize how every challenge, every decision, led us to this moment. Our next venture should embody everything we've learned."

Elena, her eyes reflecting the same passion that ignited their early days, suggests, "Our focus on social impact is a great start. Blockchain has the potential to revolutionize so many sectors – healthcare, education, governance. We can be at the forefront of this change."

Tom, always the pragmatist, adds, "While we explore these new avenues, let's not forget the lessons from our past – especially about security and user trust. Whatever we build next, it needs to be secure, transparent, and user-centric."

As they brainstorm, Jeff joins them, bringing his wisdom and experience to the table. "The blockchain world is ever-evolving. You've shown remarkable adaptability and resilience. Keep these as your guiding principles, and you'll continue to succeed."

The narrative then transitions to a series of scenes showing the trio diving into their new project. They conduct research, collaborate with experts in various fields, and engage with their community to understand the needs and possibilities of blockchain technology.

In one such collaborative session, a community leader, Mrs. Patel, who works in education, expresses her excitement about the trio's interest in educational applications of blockchain. "Your expertise could revolutionize the way we approach learning and educational records. I'm thrilled about the potential collaboration."

The trio also revisits their roots, organizing community events and workshops, not just to educate but also to gather insights and ideas from diverse groups. These events become a breeding ground for innovation and community engagement.

The trio is seen in their office late at night, surrounded by whiteboards filled with ideas, plans, and a renewed sense of purpose.

Alex, reflecting on their journey, says, "We started with a simple idea, and it grew into something beyond our wildest dreams. Our next stage is about using our knowledge, our resources, and our network to make a tangible difference in the world."

Elena, looking at the plans, adds, "We're not just part of the blockchain community; we're helping to lead it. Our journey continues, and the possibilities are limitless."
Tom, with a smile, concludes, "We've come full circle, but the journey doesn't end. It's just a new beginning."

In the closing scene, set in a quiet corner of their bustling office, Alex, Elena, and Tom gather for a moment of introspection and forward planning.

The room is filled with the energy of past achievements and the promise of future endeavors.

Alex, looking at his partners, starts, "When we began, we were driven by curiosity and a passion for technology. Now, we're leaders in a field that has the power to change the world."

Elena, with a reflective tone, adds, "Our journey has taught us so much – about technology, about business, but most importantly, about ourselves and our potential to make a difference."

Tom, who has always kept the team grounded, says, "We've had our share of challenges, but each one has brought us closer and made us stronger. I can't wait to see what the future holds for us."

Their conversation turns to the planning of their latest project, focusing on leveraging blockchain technology for social good. They discuss potential partnerships, technological challenges, and the impact they aim to achieve.

Alex shares his vision, "This new project isn't just a business venture; it's a mission. We have the opportunity to use blockchain for empowerment and positive change. Let's make sure we do it right."

Elena, always keen on innovation, suggests, "And let's keep pushing the boundaries of what's possible with blockchain. There's so much untapped potential. We can be pioneers in uncovering it."

Tom, looking at some project notes, adds, "As we embark on this new adventure, let's remember the lessons from our past. Staying true to our values has brought us this far and will guide us into the future."

The scene shifts to a montage of the trio engaging in various activities – researching, brainstorming, meeting with collaborators, and leading community workshops. Their enthusiasm and commitment are evident in every interaction.

Alex stands at a podium at a major international blockchain event. He addresses a captivated audience, sharing the story of their journey, the challenges they've overcome, and their vision for the future.

Alex concludes his speech and the chapter, "Our story is one of discovery, resilience, and innovation. We've come full circle, but our journey is far from over. The world of blockchain is vast and ever-evolving, and we're excited to continue exploring it. The future is bright, and we're just getting started."

The evening unfolds in the startup's office, now a hub of innovation and collaboration. Alex, Elena, and Tom gather for a moment of reflection and celebration with their team.

Alex addresses the team, "What we've built together is more than a company. It's a testament to what passion, hard work, and innovation can achieve. Each one of you has been integral to our journey."

Elena, looking around at the team, adds, "We've seen the power of blockchain to connect and empower. Our next projects will push these boundaries even further. The impact we can have is limitless."

Tom, holding a glass of champagne, raises a toast, "To a journey that's taken us from a humble garage to the forefront of a technological revolution. To the challenges we've overcome and the adventures that await us."

The team raises their glasses in a toast, celebrating their past achievements and the exciting prospects ahead.
The narrative then transitions to a montage sequence:

Alex, Elena, and Tom at various international conferences, sharing their knowledge and inspiring the next generation of blockchain enthusiasts.

Scenes of their new blockchain projects being implemented, showing their impact in areas like education, healthcare, and governance.

The team expanding, with new faces joining, bringing fresh ideas and energy.

Community workshops where they educate and engage with people from all walks of life, spreading the knowledge and potential of blockchain.

As the montage ends, we return to the office where Alex, Elena, and Tom are looking at a wall displaying photos of their journey – from their early days of mining to their latest achievements.

Alex, with a sense of pride and optimism, reflects, "When we started this journey, we didn't know where it would take us. Now, I see that our potential is only limited by our imagination. The world of blockchain is our canvas, and we'll continue to paint it with innovation and integrity."

Elena, looking at the photos, smiles, "These memories are just the beginning. Our journey has been incredible, but I have a feeling our greatest achievements are yet to come."

Tom, joining in, concludes, "We started with a byte, and we've built something extraordinary. Here's to the future and all the possibilities it holds. The adventure continues."

The End.

Author's Reflections

Bridging Futures: The Promise of Cryptocurrency and Blockchain

The author steps away from the narrative of Alex, Elena, and Tom to reflect on the broader implications and future possibilities of cryptocurrencies and blockchain technology. This section explores how government inclusion, support, and the ideals of human togetherness can be enhanced through decentralized systems.

Author's Reflections:

As the author of "Byte Rich: The Bitcoin Odyssey," I have journeyed alongside Alex, Elena, and Tom through the labyrinth of blockchain and cryptocurrencies. This adventure has not only been a tale of technological conquest and entrepreneurial spirit but also a narrative that mirrors the immense potential and the challenges facing the world of digital currencies and blockchain technology.

Government Inclusion and Support:

One of the most significant developments in the blockchain space is the evolving stance of governments worldwide. Initially met with skepticism, blockchain technology is now being recognized for its potential in creating transparent, efficient, and secure systems. Governments are gradually moving from a position of caution to one of exploration, with some even adopting blockchain in areas such as digital identity verification, voting systems, and public record management.

The promise of government inclusion in blockchain initiatives signifies a monumental shift. When state mechanisms decide to integrate blockchain technology, it symbolizes a bridge between traditional governance and futuristic technology. This integration has the potential to streamline bureaucratic processes, reduce corruption, and increase public trust in governmental operations.

The Promise of New Cryptocurrencies:

As we've seen with Bitcoin, Ethereum, and other cryptocurrencies, these digital assets are more than just tools for investment. They represent a new paradigm in how we perceive value, transactional processes, and financial autonomy. The emergence of new cryptocurrencies, especially those focusing on specific utilities beyond mere trading, is set to revolutionize various sectors.

We are stepping into an era where cryptocurrencies could facilitate everything from microtransactions in developing economies to large-scale financial operations in the corporate world. The flexibility and security offered by these digital currencies promise a more inclusive financial system, one where access is not limited by geographical boundaries or traditional banking limitations.

Ideals for Human Togetherness:

Perhaps the most profound impact of decentralized blockchain technology lies in its ability to foster human togetherness and cooperation. In a world often divided by physical and digital borders, blockchain stands as a unifying force. Its very nature – decentralized, transparent, and based on consensus – encourages collaborative efforts and trust-building among diverse groups.

Blockchain technology can help create a world where transactions, agreements, and records are transparent and immutable, fostering a sense of fairness and trust among participants. This transparency can bridge gaps in understanding and cooperation, leading to a more connected and cohesive global society.

Improving Lives Through Decentralization:

The decentralized nature of blockchain paves the way for more equitable and user-centric systems. From decentralized finance (DeFi) platforms offering banking services to the unbanked, to decentralized autonomous organizations (DAOs) allowing for more democratic business operations, blockchain empowers individuals to take control of their financial and professional destinies.

In summary, as we move forward, the integration of cryptocurrencies and blockchain technology into various aspects of our lives holds the promise of a more connected, transparent, and equitable world. The journey of Alex, Elena, and Tom is a microcosm of this larger movement – a testament to the potential of blockchain to not just enrich our lives but to fundamentally transform them for the better.

The Broader Narrative:

The journey of our protagonists is emblematic of a larger movement within the technological and financial landscapes. Their experiences, challenges, and triumphs mirror the evolution of blockchain technology from a niche interest to a cornerstone of future digital infrastructures. This book is not just their story; it's the story of countless innovators, entrepreneurs, and visionaries who are shaping the blockchain revolution.

Implications for the Future:

As we look ahead, the promise of blockchain and cryptocurrencies extends into virtually every domain of our lives. From creating more inclusive financial systems to revolutionizing supply chain management, the potential applications are vast and varied. This technology could redefine how we interact with the digital world, ensuring more secure, transparent, and efficient processes.

The Role of Community and Collaboration:

A recurring theme in "Byte Rich" is the power of community and collaboration. The blockchain ethos is deeply rooted in these principles – decentralized networks thrive on collective participation and consensus. This book underscores the importance of building and nurturing communities that can drive innovation and foster trust in new technologies.

Challenges and Responsibilities:

With great power comes great responsibility. The narrative of "Byte Rich" doesn't shy away from addressing the challenges and ethical considerations that come with blockchain technology. Issues like cybersecurity, regulatory compliance, and environmental impact are integral to the discourse surrounding blockchain and cryptocurrencies. As we forge ahead, balancing innovation with responsibility remains paramount.

A Call to Action:

"Byte Rich: The Bitcoin Odyssey" concludes with a call to action – an invitation to readers to engage with, contribute to, and shape the future of blockchain technology. Whether you're a developer, entrepreneur, investor, or simply a curious observer, there's a role for everyone in this evolving landscape.

Final Thoughts:

As the story of Alex, Elena, and Tom comes to a close, their journey represents just the beginning of a much larger narrative. "Byte Rich" is a window into a future where blockchain and cryptocurrencies are integral to our digital lives, offering a glimpse of the exciting possibilities that lie ahead. The book closes, leaving readers with a sense of optimism and a challenge to be part of this groundbreaking journey into the future.

"Byte Rich: The Bitcoin Odyssey" is more than a story; it's a reflection of our times and a foresight into a future where technology empowers, unites, and transforms. As we close this book, the odyssey continues, inviting each of us to be a part of this thrilling and uncharted journey.

BITCOIN WHITE PAPER

The Bitcoin whitepaper, titled "Bitcoin: A Peer-to-Peer Electronic Cash System," was published by an individual (or group) under the pseudonym Satoshi Nakamoto in 2008. It outlines the conceptual framework for the digital currency Bitcoin. Here's a summary of the key points covered in the whitepaper:

Summary of the Bitcoin Whitepaper

1. Introduction:

Nakamoto introduces the fundamental problem with traditional online transactions: the reliance on trust. The paper proposes a solution to what is known as the double-spending problem through a peer-to-peer network.

2. Transactions:

The concept of an electronic coin as a chain of digital signatures is introduced. Each owner transfers the coin to the next by digitally signing a hash of the previous transaction and the public key of the next owner, adding these to the end of the coin.

3. Timestamp Server:

To counteract the issue of double-spending, the paper proposes a timestamp server that takes a hash of a block of items and publicly announces the timestamp. This helps to establish the chronological order of transactions.

4. Proof-of-Work:

The whitepaper introduces a proof-of-work system to implement the distributed timestamp server on a peer-to-peer basis. This system involves scanning for a value that when hashed, such as with SHA-256, the hash begins with a number of zero bits. The average work required increases exponentially with the number of zero bits required but can be verified quickly by executing a single hash.

5. Network:

It describes how the network operates by detailing steps on how new transactions are broadcasted, how nodes can work to extend the proof-of-work chain, and how they can reach a consensus on the longest proof-of-work chain as proof of what happened while they were gone.

6. Incentive:

Nakamoto discusses how new coins can be introduced into the system. The paper suggests giving nodes that generate new blocks (miners) a reward in the form of new transaction fees and new coins, an incentive that ensures honest nodes stay motivated to support the network.

7. Reclaiming Disk Space:

To allow for efficient use of disk space, the whitepaper suggests a method where old transactions can be compacted, requiring only the root of a Merkle tree of transactions in a block, reducing the amount of data that needs to be stored.

8. Simplified Payment Verification:

It's possible to verify payments without running a full network node. A user only needs to keep a copy of the block headers of the longest proof-of-work chain, which can be used to check the validity of transactions.

9. Combining and Splitting Value:

Transactions can contain multiple inputs and outputs, allowing for more flexibility in the system. This enables splitting and combining value, making it possible to aggregate several transactions into one.

10. Privacy:

The paper discusses privacy within the system, noting that while the public nature of the blockchain makes it public, privacy can still be maintained by keeping public keys anonymous.

11. Calculations:

The final section discusses the probability of an attacker catching up with the honest chain as a Poisson distribution and concludes that as long as honest nodes control the majority of CPU power on the network, they will generate the longest chain and outpace attackers.

Conclusion

The Bitcoin whitepaper presents a groundbreaking approach to creating a decentralized digital currency. It addresses major challenges related to trust and double-spending in digital transactions, proposing a novel solution that has led to the development of the first cryptocurrency, Bitcoin. The concepts introduced in this paper have laid the foundation for the burgeoning field of blockchain technology and cryptocurrencies.

Made in the USA
Columbia, SC
27 January 2024

30095198R00114